Incredible Coincidences

Vikas Khatree

Publishers
Pustak Mahal®

Administrative office and sale centre
J-3/16 , Daryaganj, New Delhi-110002
☎ 23276539, 23272783, 23272784 • *Fax:* 011-23260518
E-mail: info@pustakmahal.com • *Website:* www.pustakmahal.com

Branches
Bengaluru: ☎ 080-22234025 • *Telefax:* 080-22240209
E-mail: pustak@airtelmail.in • pustak@sancharnet.in
Mumbai: ☎ 022-22010941, 022-22053387
E-mail: rapidex@bom5.vsnl.net.in
Patna: ☎ 0612-3294193 • *Telefax:* 0612-2302719
E-mail: rapidexptn@rediffmail.com

ISBN 978-81-223-0935-5

Edition: 2013

Printed at : **AR Emm International Delhi**

Contents

Preface

Coincidence can be described as the chance occurrence at the same time or place of two or more events that appear to be related or similar. Coincidences are the most delightful oddities of daily life. They make us wonder about the larger pattern and greater meaning of existence. So bizarre are some occurrences that it is not possible to dismiss them as chance happening.

As the philosopher, Arthur Shopenhauer wrote, the real significance of coincidences exists only in relation to the individual who experiences them; for other people, for whom they have no significance, these coincidences pass unnoticed into the background of everyday life. For example, that a child was born at nine minutes past 9 p.m. on 9.9.99 draws disdain from the sceptics, so what? With so many children born every minute, somebody had to be. A second point to bear in mind is that coincidences are essentially random, non-repeatable events which do not 'sort' themselves; we have the big with the small, the major with the minor.

There is also a category of coincidence, which occurs to most of the people; sending a letter to someone you haven't contacted for, say, a year and receiving one back in the post next morning, obviously sent before yours arrived.

Coincidence can stimulate the level of our awareness, if we learn to recognise them for what they are, do not dismiss them lightly when they happen to us but instead pause to consider what they could be trying to tell us. That is what their "law" is. Developing such an awareness is not a difficult task. I hope this book will help in the pleasing task.

1. Twenty-one

When Louis XVI of France was a child, an astrologer warned him to be always on his guard on the 21st of every month. The advice terrified the young child, and, thereafter, he refused to undertake any important business on that day.

In spite of his precautions in regard to business, he was caught up in larger events on that date. It was on June 21, 1791, that Louis and his queen were arrested at Varennes as they tried to escape the revolution. On September 21, the following year, France abolished monarchy and proclaimed itself a republic. On January 21, 1793, Louis XVI was executed.

2. Cloudy Meetings

George Best was a private with the Sherwood Foresters in the First World War. He and another soldier from the regiment were fleeing the Germans, when the other man slipped and ended up face-down in the mud.

Best helped his colleague to sit up. He had hurt his ankle and told Best to leave him. With the Germans closing in, it was the obvious thing to do. In the end, however, both were captured, although sent to different POW camps.

Best, in fact, escaped three times, and bore a small scar on his face for the rest of his life, a reminder of the rifle butt a German guard had smashed into his face.

In 1929, Best and his wife were visiting relatives in Leicester for Christmas. The ex-soldier and one of the male relatives went to a football match. As the one-sided match drew to a close, they joined the growing exodus. Suddenly, there was a commotion behind him and Best turned to see a man had slipped and was lying face down in the mud. Best bent to assist the man and found himself looking at the soldier he had last seen in that position shortly before the two of them were captured in 1917.

3. The Subway that Stopped

It was November 1971 in London on a day like any other. In one of the city's subway station, a train was approaching the platform. Suddenly, a young man hurled himself directly into the path of the moving train. The horrified driver applied the brakes, certain that there was no way to stop the train before the man was crushed under the wheels. But miraculously, the train did stop. The first carriage had to be jacked up to remove the badly injured man, but the wheels had not passed over him and he survived.

The young man turned out to be a gifted architect recovering from a nervous breakdown. His amazing rescue from death was based on coincidence. The investigation of the accident revealed that the train had not stopped because of the driver's hasty braking.

Seconds before, acting on an impulse and completely unaware of the man about to throw himself on the tracks, a passenger had pulled down the emergency handle, which automatically applied the brakes of the train. The passenger had no particular reason for doing so. In fact, the transport authority considered prosecuting him on the grounds that he had had no reasonable cause for using the emergency system!

4. Nursing Other's Daughter

By a tragic coincidence, the two girls, who were injured in a bad car crash near Seville in Spain looked remarkably similar. One girl later died. The other, terribly scarred and with facial injuries, lived, but suffered from loss of memory as a result of the accident.

The parents of the one girl were grief-stricken and went into deep mourning, while the other couple prepared themselves for the long fight to help their daughter to get back to normal. As she recovered, the sickening truth dawned on them — she was not their daughter. In the confusion of the accident, the hospital had mixed up the girls' handbags, and, as a result, their identification.

Two months after the crash in 1978, the grieving family was re-united with the daughter it thought it had lost. The patience and love of the other family turned to despair when it learnt that it had been nursing someone else's daughter — and it was theirs who had been buried.

5. Great Grandmother

A graveside funeral service was held up for half-an-hour when the vicar realised he was burying the wrong body. He noticed, as wreaths were removed from the coffin top, that it bore a man's name — and not that of great-grandmother Nora Boote.

Relatives waited in the church while embarrassed funeral directors rushed off to collect Mrs Boote's body and coffin so that the service at St Michael's Church in Bishops Hitchington, Warwickshire, could continue.

6. Adams and Jefferson

Thomas Jefferson was the author of the Declaration of Independence, and John Adams was one of its chief promulgators. Adams became the second president of the United

States and Jefferson, the third. The two men died in the same year, 1826, and on the same days, the 50th anniversary of the most important day in their lives: July 4. Jefferson apparently willed himself to live until then. Before breathing his last, he asked whether it was the fourth. Adams, whose famous last words were "Thomas Jefferson still survives," outlived his compatriot by only five hours.

7. Arrested In-flight

In early 1988, drugs squad detective Peter Miller arrested Stephen Rotaru, thirty-one, from Cleveland, Ohio, on charges of supplying and possessing cocaine and possessing cannabis leaf. Three weeks after the arrest, Miller went on holidays. At Sydney airport, Miller boarded Continental Flight 16, bound for Ohio via Miller's destination, Hawaii. As he made his way down the aisle, he saw Rotaru in a seat. Miller promptly rearrested the American. Rotaru had surrendered his passport after originally being arrested, but had then persuaded the US

Consulate to issue him with a new one. Miller was not consciously searching in any manner for Rotaru. As far as he was concerned, the American, who hotly protested his innocence, fully intended to stand trial.

In addition to surrendering the passport, he had put up bail and was reporting to a police station twice a week. Miller had booked on the same flight for no other reason than he wanted to go to Hawaii for a holiday.

8. Hot Tips

On 9th July 1981, the day Prince Charles and Lady Diana married, a quarter of the horse-races in Britain were won by starters with names such as Tender King, Favoured Lady and Wedded Bliss.

Of the 200 horses, that ran that day, eleven had 'royal' or other suitable names and, of those, six won or came second in seventeen races at combined odds of 54,000 to one against such an occurrence, and not one was a favourite.

9. Doppelganger

Private Bill Spencer found himself wandering aimlessly through the streets of Adelaide. Instead of enjoying his twenty-four-hour leave, he was feeling, for reasons he could not fathom, strangely uneasy.

He had an early evening meal and was killing time until he could attend a film or a dance and then return to his antiaircraft battery at Outer Harbour, on the outskirts of Adelaide.

In Rundle street, which was in 1945 the main shopping centre, he paused and something made him glance back towards the intersection with King William Street. He noticed a military policeman there with another soldier.

As the two men spoke, they were looking at him and obviously the conversation was about him. He expected the MP to approach and ask for his leave pass. As it was in order, he was not concerned and made no attempt to move away. However, it was the soldier who approached.

Standing directly in front of Bill, he said: 'Good day.'

Bill responded uncertainly: 'Good day.'

The soldier was surprised at Bill's lack of enthusiasm. 'Don't you remember me?'

Bill said he had never seen him before in his life. At this, the other soldier became agitated. 'You must remember me. We were in the same tent for six weeks in Rottnest.' Rottnest is a tiny island off Western Australia.

Bill took a step back and told the other soldier: 'I've never seen you before and I've never been out of South Australia in my life.'

Then, to Bill's amazement, the man said: 'You're Bill Spencer, aren't you?'

Bill agreed he was.

At this the soldier became insistent. The same tent. Six weeks. Same name. Why didn't he want to admit knowing him? What was wrong?

As the soldier grew more upset, Bill was at a loss. All he could do was stand by what he had said earlier.

Eventually, the other man calmed down and went on his way, still obviously thinking he had run into the Bill Spencer he had known on Rottnest.

In 1948, Bill happened to move to Western Australia, where he still lives. He made several attempts to find the man who was both his namesake and look alike, but without success. At first, he assumed the other Bill Spencer had been killed in the last few months of hostilities or had moved elsewhere. But then people started telling him they had seen him in places he knew he had not been. "Saw you in Perth today, or Victoria Park, or the beach". This had gone on for years. He has made a number of appeals through the WA media, but without success.

'I would like to have found this other Bill Spencer who looks so much like me,' Bill remarked. 'But I'm going on for seventy-six, so there's not much hope now.'

10. What a Duplicate?

On July 28, 1900, King Umberto I of Italy and his aide-de-camp Gen. Emilio Ponzio-Vaglia arrived in the town of Monza, a few miles outside Milan. The next day, the king was to present the prizes at an athletic meet. On the night of their arrival, he and his aide went to a small restaurant for dinner. As the owner was taking their order, the king noticed that he and the padrone were virtually doubles, in both face and build. He remarked on this, and as the two men talked, an extraordinary series of parallels emerged which startled them.

The king was staggered by these coincidences and asked the restaurateur how it could be that their paths had never before crossed? In fact, Umberto told him, they had been decorated for bravery together on two occasions, the first time in 1866, when Umberto had been a private and the king colonel, and the second time in 1870 when each had been promoted to sergeant and corps commander. With this final revelation, the padrone returned to his duties, and the king, turning to his aide, said, "I intend to make that man a Cavaliere of the Crown of Italy tomorrow. Be sure he comes to the meet.

The following day, true to his word, the king asked for his double only to be told that the man had died that day in a shooting accident. Shocked, the king asked his aide to find out when the funeral was to take place so that he might attend. At that very moment, three shots rang out, fired by an assassin. The first of them missed the king, but the second two pierced his heart and killed him instantly.

11. An Obligation Paid

One day in 1952, a navy flyer, William Riordan, was driving home from the naval air base where he was stationed when he noticed that cars on the road ahead were slowing down. As he approached, he saw that they were avoiding something lying near the narrow pavement. When he came alongside, he saw a man proning on the ground.

While other drivers blasted their horns in objection to his slowing down traffic to help what they called "a sleeping drunk," he pulled his car off the road and stopped to investigate. He found that the man had a large scalp wound that couldn't be seen from the road. After giving the man first aid, the flyer sent for an ambulance. When it had taken the man away, he went home and forgot the incident.

Several months later, the pilot was flying over the same area in a blinding snowstorm. The air intakes on three of the plane's engines became clogged with snow, causing a power failure. The plane crashed in the woods near the air base.

When the navy ambulance arrived at the scene, they found the pilot hanging by his legs from a jagged piece of steel. The sharp edges had cut through his legs to the bones, but a man was standing under the flyer, holding him up, so his legs would not be completely torn off by the weight of his body. The man said he had been supporting the pilot like that for about an hour.

After they cut the flyer away from the wreckage, he regained consciousness for a time and discovered that the man, who had saved his legs, was the one he had aided alongside the road.

12. Playwright's Premonition

In the 1880s, Arthur Law had written a play in which the sole survivor of a shipwrecked vessel, the *Caroline,* was called Robert Golding. Within days of the play's first performance, he read a newspaper story about a real shipwreck in which there had been only one survivor. The name of the ship, the *Caroline*; the name of the survivor, Robert Golding.

13. The Spirit of a Child

Film star Julie Christie appeared in the movie, *Don't Look Now,* in which she and her screen husband (Donald Sutherland) are haunted by the spirit of their young child, who has drowned in a shallow pond at their English country house.

Some years later, Christie was visiting her farmhouse in Wales, looked after by a married couple, when the husband found the body of their twenty-two-month-old son floating in the large duckpond near the house. Christie waded in to recover the body from the shallow pond, just as the father (Sutherland) had done in the film.

14. Adoption Anniversary

Augustus J. C. Hare, a well-known writer and artist in the Victorian period, had been given up for adoption in the 1830's when he was only 14 months old. Following his graduation from Oxford, he lived mainly in Europe, making occasional visits to England. In his autobiography, Hare tells the following story:

> On the anniversary of my adoption, we all went over to Mannheim, and dined at the hotel where, seventeen years before, I, being fourteen months old, was given away to my aunt, who was also my godmother, to live with her forever as if I were her own child. . . . When we returned to the station in the evening . . . on the platform was a poor woman, crying very bitterly, with a little child in her arms. Emmie Penrhyn . . . went up to her and said she was afraid she was in some great trouble. "Yes," she said.

"It is about my 14-month-old child, who is going away from me forever in the train which is coming, to be adopted by his aunt, who is also his godmother, and I shall never, never have anything to do with him any more."

15. The Capuchin Monk

When Joseph Aigner, who became a well-known portrait painter, was 18 years old, he tried to hang himself but was prevented by the mysterious arrival of a Capuchin monk. This took place in Vienna in 1836. Four years later, in Budapest, Aigner again tried to hang himself and was again prevented by the sudden appearance of the same monk. Eight years went by and Aigner, who had espoused a revolutionary cause, was sentenced to the gallows for his political activities. He was reprieved, however, at the intervention of a monk — the same Capuchin. Finally, in 1886 when he was 68 years old, Aigner fulfilled his death wish and killed himself with a pistol. His funeral ceremony was conducted by the Capuchin monk, whose name, to the very last, Aigner had never learned.

16. 7onald 7eagan

According to Robert Ripley in *The Book of Chances* (1989), ex-President Ronald Reagan saved seventy-seven people from drowning during his seven years as a lifeguard at a resort near Dixon, Illinois. The book uses this as a starting point to show how the number 7 kept cropping up in Reagan's life.

He celebrated his seventieth birthday seventeen days after his first inauguration; he was wounded by the would be assassin

John Hinckley on his seventieth day in office, the bullet fired by Hinckley ricocheting off Reagan's seventh rib.

Reagan made his film debut in 1937 and became president of the Screen Actors' Guild in 1947. He began his term as Governor of California in 1967 and was re-elected in 1970. His formal acceptance speech for the Republican presidential nomination was made on the seventeenth day of the seventh month in 1980. At the end of his second term in the White House, he was seventy-seven.

17. One Good Tourniquet ...

One June night in the 1930's, Allan Falby, captain of the El Paso County Highway Patrol, was in hot pursuit of a speeding truck in El Paso County, Texas. The truck slowed to take a corner, and Falby rammed into it at full speed. The collision ruptured an artery in his leg, and if Alfred Smith had not stopped to give him first aid, he would certainly have died. As it was, the tourniquet that Smith applied stopped the blood flow and an ambulance reached Falby in time to save his life and his leg. After several months in a hospital, Falby was well enough to return to his job.

Five years later, Falby was again on night patrol when he received a radio message to assist at a bad accident on U.S.80. A car had smashed into a tree, and the man was in critical condition. Falby arrived at the scene before the ambulance and found an unconscious man in the car; he had severed an artery in his right leg and was bleeding to death. Falby applied a tourniquet and managed to stop the bleeding. Then he stared at the victim: it was, of course, Alfred Smith.

"It all goes to prove," Falby said later, "that one good tourniquet deserves another."

18. Ghost of the Air

Martin Caidin, in his book, *Ghost of the Air* (1991), tells of a letter he received in which Captain Robert Tyler relates this story:

I was flying F-100s in the United Kingdom right after pilot training and, like all good fighter pilots, liked to make the rounds of the English pubs. One night, shortly before closing, I had an uncontrollable urge to go outside and into a local cemetery. To this day, I don't know why, because I don't like cemeteries, and especially, wouldn't normally go to one at night.

In any event, I was drawn outside and found myself looking at headstones in the moonlight. In fact, I was unerringly drawn to one particular headstone which read: Flt Lt. Robert Tyler, RAF, downed flying Spitfires during the Battle of Britain, 15th September, 1940.

Captain Tyler had been born on 15th September, 1940.

19. Brawn Hotel

Dr. Warren Weaver tells the following story in his book, *Lady Luck: The Theory of Probability*. The probable date was the late 90's:

My next-door neighbour, Mr. George D. Bryson, was making a business trip, some years ago from St. Louis to New York. This involved weekend travel and he was in no hurry. He had never been to Louisville, Kentucky, and was interested in seeing the town. Since his train passed through Louisville, he asked the conductor, after he had boarded the train, whether he might have a stopover at Louisville.

This was possible, and on arrival at Louisville, he enquired at the station for the leading hotel. He, accordingly, went to the Brawn Hotel and registered. And then, just as a lark, he stepped up to the mail desk and asked if there was any mail for him.

The girl calmly handed him a letter addressed to "Mr. George D. Bryson, Room 307," that being the number of the room to which he had just been assigned.

It turned out that the preceding resident of Room 307 was another George D. Bryson, who was associated with an insurance company in Montreal but came originally from North Carolina. The two Mr. Brysons eventually met, so each could pinch the other to be sure he was real.

20. Unforgettable Number

Donald Baird has never forgotten this bizarre coincidence, even though it happened to him more than fifty years ago. He had enlisted with the RAF as aircrew and was posted to Winnipeg,

Canada, for training. Shortly after he arrived, he visited the airmen's club, a social meeting place for the enlisted men and local people. A young woman with whom he was dancing invited him to her parents' house for dinner on his next leave. She gave him her telephone number: 403706.

Baird wondered for a moment if she was trying to pull his leg. His air-force number was 403706. But she wasn't and for the next three months he found himself dialling his own number.

The coincidences continued. The woman's name was Jan Crawford, and she had a sister called Eleanor. The name of the girlfriend Baird had left behind was June Crawford, whose sister was also Eleanor. Finally, the airman's club in Winnipeg was in Donald Street.

21. First Passerby

In 1858, Robert Fallon, of Northumberland, England, was accused of cheating in a poker game at the Bella Union saloon in San Francisco and shot dead. Since money won by cheating—$600 in this case—was thought to be unlucky, the other players called in the first available passerby to take the dead man's place, confident that they would soon win the money back. By the time the police arrived, the new player had turned the original $600 into $2,200. When the police asked for the $600, so that they could pass it on to the dead man's next of kin, the young stranger proved that he was Fallon's son, who had not seen his father for seven years.

22. Yankee Prisoners

During the Civil War, a group of Yankee prisoners was being transferred by train to a prison camp in Salisbury, North Carolina. One of the guards on the train was a 17-year-old named Beverley Tucker, and his duty was to guard a number of prisoners who spent the journey whispering together in a foreign language. As it turned out, they were speaking the dialect of their native Swiss canton and were plotting their escape. At a way station, they made their bid for freedom - and found themselves encircled by the bayonets of the guards. They had the misfortune to be put in the charge of Bev Tucker - probably the only man in the entire Confederate Army who understood their language. He had gone to school in their native canton.

23. A Jinxed Train

On 24th August 1983, the Amtrak Silver Meteor train set out on its regular run from Miami to New York. At 7.40 p.m., in Savannah, the train struck and killed a woman who was fishing from a bridge. At 9.30 p.m., just twenty-seven kilometres further on, it hit and destroyed a truck parked close to the lines in Ridgeland. The crewmen were so shaken by the two events that rail officials decided to replace them.

At 1.10 a.m., the following morning, the train hit a tractor-trailer on a crossing at Rowland, and two passenger cars were derailed, sending twenty-one people to a hospital — including the engine driver. Once again, Amtrak officials brought in a new crew and the train continued its journey. At 2.37 a.m. in Kenly, it ran headlong into a car that ignored the warning lights at another crossing.

The National Transport Safety Board then stepped in. They had no reason to doubt the quality of the machinery or question the competence of the crews. So they declared Amtrak 117 to be a 'rogue train' and cancelled the rest of the journey.

24. Lincoln and Kennedy

Two of the most tragic and dramatic deaths in American history, the assassinations of Presidents Abraham Lincoln and John Fitzgerald Kennedy, involve the following astonishing parallels:

1) Lincoln was elected president in 1860. Exactly one hundred years later, in 1960, Kennedy was elected president.
2) Both men were deeply involved in civil rights for Negroes.
3) Both men were assassinated on a Friday, in the presence of their wives.
4) Each wife had lost a son while living at the White House.
5) Both men were killed by a bullet that entered the head from behind.

6) Lincoln was killed in Ford's Theatre. Kennedy met his death while riding in a Lincoln convertible made by the Ford Motor Company.

7) Both men were succeeded by vice presidents named Johnson who were southern Democrats and former senators.

8) Andrew Johnson was born in 1808. Lyndon Johnson was born in 1908, exactly one hundred years later.

9) The first name of Lincoln's private secretary was John, the last name of Kennedy's private secretary was Lincoln.

10) John Wilkes Booth was born in 1839 (according to some sources). Lee Harvey Oswald was born in 1939, one hundred years later.

11) Both assassins were Southerners who held extremist views.

12) Both assassins were murdered before they could be brought to trial.

13) Booth shot Lincoln in a theatre and fled to a barn. Oswald shot Kennedy from a warehouse and fled to a theatre.
14) LINCOLN and KENNEDY each has seven letters.
15) ANDREW JOHNSON and LYNDON JHOHNSON each has 13 letters.
16) JOHN WILKES BOOTH and LEE HARVEY OSWALD each had 15 letters.

In addition, the first public proposal that Lincoln be the Republican candidate for president (in a letter to the Cincinnati Gazette, November 6, 1858) also endorsed a John Kennedy for vice president (John P. Kennedy, formally secretary of the navy).

25. Golden Pen

Ms Patricia Weston was deputy principal of a high school in the town of Bunbury, Western Australia, in 1977. She asked a friend, Barry Smith, from Perth, the state capital, to partner her at the school's annual ball. They went to a local restaurant for dinner before the dance. Afterwards, as he changed from his dinner jacket, he noticed he had lost his gold pen.

Next morning, they went back to the ballroom. Failing to locate the pen there, they tried the restaurant, where its owner was pleased to return the gold Schaeffer, which was easily identified as it had 'B. Smith' inscribed on it.

That evening Barry was packing his case to return to Perth when he found his pen in the bag. Somewhat wonderingly, he went to his jacket pocket, when he had put it that morning.

Another pen. He now had two, both inscribed 'B. Smith'!

Barry left the "returned" pen with Patricia just in case somebody claimed it, but nobody ever did.

A similar case: In 1953, Boone Aiken lost his pen in Florence, South Carolina. Like Barry Smith's pen, it was engraved with his name. Three years later, Boone and his wife were in New York. As Mrs Aiken left their hotel, she saw a pen lying in the street that looked familiar. It was her husband's, as the engraving clearly showed.

26. Generation Gap

The author, J. Bryan III describes a curious bridging of time and space that occurred around 1960 when he was in Majorca writing about the American Civil War:

I finished my book. The very last passage I typed was the inscription on a tablet that stands on my grandfather's old place:

"At this point, where the intermediate line of the Richmond defences cross Brooke Road, Confederate forces on March 1, 1864, repulsed Kilpatricks raid, undertaken to release federal prisoners in Richmond ......"

That done, I bundled up the manuscript, left it at the post office and drove to a luncheon given by some Austrian friends. I arrived late; the party consisting of 16 or 18 people was already moving towards the dinning room. I knew scarcely a soul, but there was not much time for introductions. I slid into my chair and was about to take a tranquillising swallow of wine when the hostess announced to those at their end of the table, "Mr. Bryan here is from Richmond."

The gentleman sitting across me said pleasantly, "Richmond? I've often wanted to go there, but at the last minute something has always prevented it." He smiled, then went on. "Come to think of it, my grandfather had the same experience."

I have no explanation for what I said next, except that the inscription I had just transcribed was fresh in my subconscious. I asked, "Is your name Kilpatrick, sir?"

"No," he said, "but my grandfather's was," he was that Kilpatrick, too!

Savour it for a moment—the two of us meeting on a small island in the Mediterranean and discovering that 6400 kms away and almost a hundred years before, his grandfather had been "repulsed" from my grandfather's place in a minor skirmish of the Civil war!

27. It Finished Seven

The following memoir, sent to Arthur Koestler after the publication of his book, *The Roots of Coincidence* in 1973, may be too good to be true. The author of the letter, Anthony S. Clancy of Dublin, Ireland, writes:

I was born on the seventh day of the week, seventh day of the month, seventh month of the year, seventh year of the century. I was the seventh child of a seventh child, and I have seven brothers; that makes seven sevens. On my 27th birthday, at a race meeting, when I looked at the race card to pick a winner in the seventh race. The horse numbered seven was called Seventh Heaven, with a handicap of seven stone. The odds were seven to one. I put seven shillings on this horse. It finished seventh.

28. Fatal Car Accident

James Dean (1931-55) became a symbol of restless youth, starring in films such as *Rebel Without a Cause*. His early death in a car accident turned him into a figure around whom legends have grown. One of the first concerned the car in which he died. A mechanic who was working on the wrecked vehicle had both his legs broken when the engine slipped and fell on him. It meant he was not there when a fire damaged the workshop.

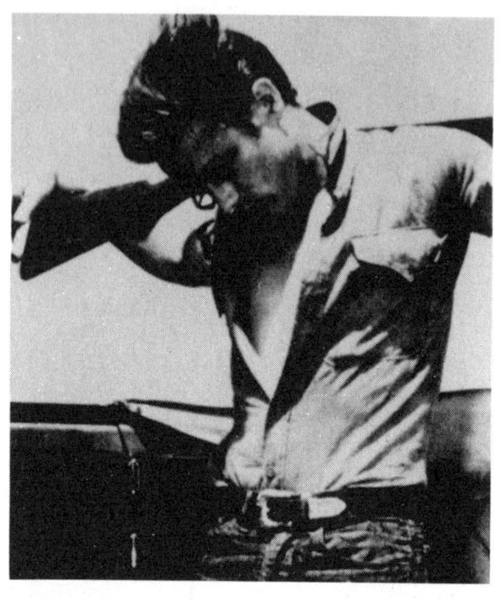

A doctor eventually bought the engine and had it installed in his racing car. He died in a race shortly afterwards. Another driver had the drive shaft of Dean's car installed in his car; he also died in the race.

Eventually, the car was repaired and then sold for display purposes. In Sacramento, California, it fell from its stand and broke the hip of a teenage fan. In Oregon, the truck on which it was being carried smashed through the front of a shop. In 1959, it once again slipped from its steel supports and broke into eleven pieces.

29. Tehran Club

Former British intelligence officer Arthur Seaborn was dining one evening in June 1944 at the Tehran Club in Iran with his friend Captain John Holder of the Dorsetshire regiment. At the time, John was aide-de-camp to Major General Lochner while he was on the General Staff HQ for the Persian area.

The purpose of the dinner was to celebrate Holder's engagement to a corporal in the South African Women's Auxiliary Army Service unit, stationed near Cairo.

It was a warm evening and dinner was being served in the garden, where tables were set among the trees and shrubs. On each table stood a small electric lamp in the shape of a candle, providing just sufficient light for the diner to see by.

Seaborn called a waiter and ordered a bottle of champagne. When the waiter had filled their glasses, he raised his and said: 'Well, John, here's happiness and good health to both of you.' But before they could drink the toast, an extraordinary thing happened. The candle-shaped globe of the electric light suddenly popped out of its socket and struck Seaborn's right hand, so that the wine glass was knocked almost from his grasp and its contents were spilled over the tablecloth.

They sat there dumbfounded as the waiter hurried to the rescue, removed the soiled tablecloth and relaid the table, carefully replacing the offending lamp globe in its socket. Seaborn was given a clean glass, which the waiter immediately refilled. Again he raised his glass and began to repeat the toast.

Half way through the second toast everything happened as before. The globe popped out of its socket, only this time it hit and shattered Seaborn's glass.

Holder was considerably shaken, insisting that he was superstitious enough to believe that this startling occurrence was a bad omen for his forthcoming marriage. Seaborn thought that he was not feeling too happy about it either. He tried to allay the other man's fears, but was not surprised when Holder forbade him from attempting the toast, a third time.

Next morning at HQ, an ashen-faced Holder walked into Seaborn's office. He was holding a signal form. The gist of its message was that a military transport plane carrying service personnel from Alexandria to Haifa had crashed the previous day near Cairo at 2015 hours (8.15 p.m.). There were no survivors. Holder's fiancée had been one of the passengers.

They had ordered dinner at the Tehran Club for 8 p.m., but had sat down five minutes late. By the time, the waiter had brought the bottle of champagne and filled the glasses, it had been right on 8.15 — the exact moment the plane had crashed!

30. Optimistic Expectations

Everyone, from time to time, experiences one of those perfect days when everything seems to fall into place, a day that exceeds the most optimistic expectations — the kind of day that persuades one that one's guardian angel is working overtime. One of the most extraordinary of these "perfect days' is recorded by Prof. C. E. Sherman, a longtime chairman of the Civil Engineering Department of Ohio State University at Columbus, in his book, *Land of Kingdom Come:*

In 1909, while preparing the originals for the Ohio State Highway Atlas, we were hard put to it to get maps of the south-western counties. . . . The United States Geological Survey had not yet mapped this area, and the only suitable data . . . to be had were in the form of old county atlases about 15 inches square and half-an-inch thick. . . .

Much correspondence had secured the data for every county in the state except Pike and Highland. These two could not be had, nor could I discover after my painstaking enquiry whether any map of these regions existed. In the absence of any data at all, it would be a tough task to make a complete survey of all the roads in a county. In fact, it was out of the question with the appropriation we had. So I left Columbus, resolved to search the county seats and the homesteads nearby, for a week or two, if necessary, to get the lost data. We also wanted a good map of the Ohio River for adjusting the data we had already gathered.

The following events then happened during the next 12 hours, that Saturday in August. Taking an early morning train for Cincinnati, I found an excellent map of the Ohio at the first place I visited, The United States Engineers Office. . . . Proceeding at once to Highland country, I had to wait at Norwood for the Hillsboro car. When I happened to mention the nature of my quest to the ticket agent at Norwood, he said, "There's an old book like that in the rear room, I think." We searched the dusty pile together and fished out the long-sought Highland County Atlas!

Two ways then offered of reaching Pike's capital that afternoon. I ate lunch and took the B.&O. [railroad] to Chillicothe. In the short wait there, for the N.&W. south, I strolled up the street to call on an old friend, if perchance he were in town. He came towards me as I started, just as if the whole thing had been prearranged. After our chat, as I was mounting the southbound train, a gentleman, who had written the day before, hailed me. As his letter was of a nature much more easily answered orally, it was gratifying to give him the immediate information.

I was personally acquainted with but two citizens of Waverly [the county seat of Pike County], one a mechanical, the other a civil engineering student, but hardly expected either of them to be in town. When I stepped off at Waverly, the mechanical engineer stepped off the car in front, and, as we walked towards the hotel together, he said he would send around the other man if he were home. I had just leisurely finished dinner at seven o'clock when Gehres appeared. Did he know of any Pike County map? "No, but perhaps father does," he said, "and here comes father now." Mr. Gehres, senior, said he thought the county auditor had one. The auditor came walking up the street as he spoke. After introductions, and in accord with the happenings of the whole day, he took us across the street to his office in the court house, where hung a fine old map of the county. I had written the county surveyor of that same county, but he knew nothing of this map.

I am actually afraid to record here all the incidents of the trip that I have on the memorandum here before me. It would be straining credulity too much. . . You see, every step taken during the day was as much to the purpose as if planned with foreknowledge. I had gone directly to the Ohio River maps . . . had gone directly to a Highland County Atlas without knowing one existed, by the shortest travelled route; and when from that point two ways might be taken, I had chosen the one that led most directly to the remaining data south.

Even the smallest incident, during the day, seemed to fit perfectly into a harmonious whole. I suppose much of this was psychological. I had for months been on the quest for all the data for the state, and when this last, hardest problem began to unravel so easily, it put me in a humour to notice only favouring circumstances, such for instance as the following:

The Norwood agent didn't want to sell, but would gladly lend his book — this saved us the purchase price. My Chillicothe friend was just leaving town on the car after, instead of the car before my arrival; again, the tracing paper I picked up at random that morning, before leaving home, just fitted the large Pike County wall map; then again, the one person that I hoped might be at home to help at Waverly if needed, was on the spot to make the Pike County tracing. Who would expect to get into the court -house in a strange town on Saturday night? Yet along came just the right persons, at just the right time, to take me to that map, which, I didn't know, existed. The train from Chillicothe to Waverly was full of men excursionists; they filled the aisles, yet as I stepped on, a seat was vacant for me, and I had uninterrupted privacy and comfort all the way down to reflect on the events of the day. I retired that night with the sensation of having experienced a perfect day.

31. Two Patients

Franz Richter, a 19-year-old volunteer in the Austrian Transport Corp following World War I, was admitted to the hospital suffering from pneumonia. In the same hospital was another patient named Franz Richter, also 19 years old, suffering from pneumonia, and a volunteer in the Transport Corps. Both men were born in Silesia.

32. Struggling Family

Over the years, three generations of the Jackson family have sailed under the colours of the Royal Australian Navy. In 1942, young sailor John Jackson was in the battle of the Coral Sea, when the combined US-Australian forces took on the might of the Japanese fleet and stopped its southward thrust.

Exactly fifty years later, his grandson, Todd, was involved in joint US-Australian commemorative exercises off the Australian coast, code-named *Operation Coral Sea*.

Todd is a Gulf War veteran and the third-generation Jackson to have been at war. His father, Peter, did five tours of Vietnam during the 1960s aboard HMAS *Sydney.*

However, it is the links between Todd and his grandfather that are most remarkable. When young Todd joined the navy on 10th January 1989, it was fifty years to the day since John Jackson had singed on. Just eighteen months after Todd joined up, he found himself getting his first taste of combat in the Gulf War. The day his ship left Fremantle, the last Australian port of call before setting out to cross the Indian Ocean for the Gulf, it was fifty years to the day since his grandfather's ship had sailed from Fremantle for Britain and his first taste of hostilities.

33. Facts and Future

In June 1957, as Norman Mailer worked on his novel, *Barbary Shore* in his New York apartment, a Soviet spy began to emerge in the plot. At first, the spy was a minor character, but as Mailer proceeded, he became a major one, eventually becoming *The* dominant character.

When the novel was finished, the FBI arrested Soviet master spy Rudolph Abel — who lived in the same apartment building as Mailer.

Mailer, like other writers, had somehow snatched both facts and the future from time and space.

34. The Duelist

Henri Tragne, of Marseille, France, fought five duels between 1861 and 1878. In the first four, his opponents fell dead before a single shot had been fired; in the fifth, Tragne himself died — again before shots had been exchanged.

35. The Unhappy Couple

The wedding day of Princess Maria del Pozzo della Cisterna, who married Amadeo, the Duke D'Aosta, the son of the king of Italy in Turin on May 30, 1867, was marred by these events:

- Her wardrobe mistress hanged herself.
- The palace gatekeeper cut his throat.

- The colonel leading the wedding procession collapsed from sunstroke.
- The station master was crushed to death under the wheels of the honeymoon train.
- The king's aide was killed by a fall from his horse.
- The best man shot himself.

The couple did not live happily everafter.

36. Similar Assassins

An assassin named Claude Volbonne murdered Baron Rodemire de Tarazone of France in 1872. Twenty-one years earlier the baron's father had also been murdered by a Claude Volbonne. The two assassins were not related.

37. The Last Tsar of Russia

In his book, *The Occult* (1971), Colin Wilson gives details of some deft detective work he did which shows that, but for a coincidence, the First World War may not have happened! It is an incredible claim. But the components build up in their usual mysterious fashion.

Wilson begins with the point that one of the two main characters in this story is Rasputin, the monk who had so much influence over the last Tsar and Tsarina of Russia. On two occasions, Rasputin successfully persuaded the Tsar not to go to war over the Balkans, which were claimed by Austria.

The other character is Archduke Franz Ferdinand of Austria, who was assassinated at Sarajevo by a young Bosnian patriot, Gabriel Princip in June 1914. As a consequence, Austria declared war on Serbia. This meant the world's destiny was in the hands of the Tsar, for he had to make up his mind whether to stand by Serbia and declare war on Austria or let the Balkans solve their own problems.

This was the point where Rasputin's further advice would make all the difference between war and peace. Unfortunately, Rasputin was not around to give advice. He had been stabbed by a would-be assassin in his home village of Pokrovskoe and hovered between life and death for weeks.

When Wilson was writing his book on Rasputin, he noted the coincidence — that Rasputin and Archduke Franz Ferdinand had been struck down about the same time. Intrigued, he set about pinning down the timing more accurately. Accounts deferred on the date when Rasputin was stabbed. Historian Sir Bernard Pares seemed to think it was Saturday, 26th June, 1941. But Maria Rasputin's book on her father states quite definitely that the stabbing took place on the following day. This was made even more likely by the fact that he was stabbed after he had returned from the church. This meant that Rasputin was stabbed *on the same day* the Archduke was shot. Maria Rasputin gives the time as shortly after 2 p.m.

As for the Archduke, he had felt certain he was going to die even before visiting Sarajevo, telling his children's tutor, 'The bullet that will kill me is already on its way.'

Shortly after 10 a.m., that Sunday, a homemade bomb was thrown at his motor car but the Archduke and his wife were uninjured. They attended a ceremony on the town hall, leaving half an hour later. It was on the drive back through Sarajevo, at about 11 a.m., that Princip, a consumptive young student involved in the earlier attempt, leant forward and fired two shots, killing the Archduke and his wife.

There are 50 degrees of longitude between Sarajevo and Pokrovskoe, so the time in the two places differs. Wilson worked out the difference. It is a simple sum: The earth passes through 360 degrees when it does a complete turn in twenty-four hours — that is, 180 degrees in twelve hours, 90 degrees in six hours, 45 degrees in three hours.

So, to turn through 50 degrees, it takes exactly three hours and twenty minutes. The Archduke Ferdinand was murdered shortly before 11 a.m. Rasputin was stabbed at 2.15 p.m., and 10.55 a.m. in Sarajevo was exactly 2.15 p.m. in Pokrovskoe.

Wilson concludes: *'The man whose death caused the First World War, and the man who could have averted the war, were struck down at the same moment.* The coincidence is as extraordinary as any, I have came across.

38. The Bank Robbery

Charles Wells was so famous that they wrote a music-hall song about him: "The Man Who Broke the Bank at Monte Carlo."

In fact, Wells broke the bank three times. He was not a wellknown gambler, he used no "system," he was not in the least bit dashing (he was, in fact, a fat Englishman), and after his staggering successes, he was never again seen in the casino.

The first two times, he broke the bank in 1891—that is, won the 100,000 francs "bank" allocated to each table—he did so by putting even-money bets on black and red and winning nearly every time. On the third occasion, he placed his opening bet on the number five, at odds of 35 to 1, and won. He left his original bet on the number, and won again. He did this five times, all told, and each time the number five came up for him, the bank was broken again and Charles Wells left quietly with his winnings.

He was said by someone, who had met him, to be a slightly sinister man.

39. Three Names

Three Englishmen travelling by rail in Peru, one day in the 1920's, found themselves to be the only occupants of their passenger car, introducing themselves, they discovered that the first man's surname was Bingham, and the second man's Powell; the third man was Bingham Powell.

40. A Baby Fall

Joseph Figlock was walking down a street in Detroit in the 1930's when a baby fell on him from a high window. A year later, the same baby fell on him again from the same window. Figlock and the baby, both survived.

41. Violent Storm

In October 1991, as a violent storm raged, Jennifer Roberts, twenty-three, was tucked up snugly in a tent reading Stephen King's book *The Dead Zone* — then lightning struck her.

The bolt entered Jennifer's body through her watchband and burned a trail down to her toes. Doctors said the only thing that saved her was the fact she had been lying on a rubber mattress — and that she had removed her brassiere.

It was an underwired bra and, because it had been jabbing into her, she had taken it off ten minutes before the lightning struck. Had Jennifer still been wearing it, the lightning would have re-energised the wire and given her heart a double jolt.

The lightning burnt a hole through the 290 pages of the novel. The book's cover is illustrated with the head of a man from which lightning bolts are flashing!

42. Registered Birth

Pregnant Jeanette Ellis of Cobbs Creek, Virginia, realised early one morning in February 1992 that her second child was suddenly on its way. She climbed into the rear seat of their Ford Taurus station wagon, while her husband, Tad, took the wheel. They did not make it to hospital before the birth. At 6.40 a.m., Jeanette gave birth to a boy in the back seat. The number plate of the car: BOY 640.

43. An Established Bond

Eric W. Smith, a metallurgist with the English Steel Company, lived in a quiet suburb of Sheffield called Ecclesall. Behind his house were woods where people used to ride, and in the spring and summer, it was Smith's habit to stroll there, enjoying the peace and quiet and collecting horse manure for his tomato plants. For this purpose, he carried with him a small dustpan and an old shopping bag.

One day in the late 1950's, as he was quietly making his way along a woodland path, pausing now and then to scoop up some manure for his tomatoes, he saw a figure slowly approaching him along the path, a man whose progress was also interrupted by stooping and shovelling. Clearly, Smith thought, here was another man who appreciated the virtues of horse manure.

Midway between the two men was a bench, and, reaching it simultaneously, they sat down. By a remarkable coincidence the stranger was carrying an oilcloth bag identical with Smith's, as well as a little dustpan. Both men, it turned out, had gone to the woods to collect manure for their tomatoes.

With a bond now established, Smith reached for his pipe and tobacco tin. The stranger also took out a pipe, and Smith offered him a fill of tobacco. "No thanks," the stranger said, "I have my own brand." He did. It was the same as Smith's.

At this point, both men had the sense that something eerie was happening to them.

"My name's Smith, " Smith said.

"So's mine," said the stranger.

"Eric Smith," said the first Smith.

"Me too," said the second Smith.

"Eric W. Smith."

"yes."

"The W stands for Wales," said number 1 Smith.

"Ah, " said number 2, "there we differ. I'm Walter."

44. Never Believe This

When TV talk show host and columnist Irv Kupcinet—"Kup" to his friends—was in London to cover the coronation of Elizabeth II in 1953, he stayed at the Savoy Hotel. In one of the drawers in his room, he was surprised to find some articles belonging to an old friend of his, the basketball impresario, Harry Hannin, then with the Harlem Globetrotters. He was

even more surprised when, two days later, he received a later from Hannin, who was staying at the Hotel Meurice in Paris just then. "You'll never believe this, "Hannin wrote, 'but I've just opened a drawer here and found a tie with your name on it."

45. Martial Art Sect

In his short life, Bruce Lee rose to international stardom with a series of martial arts films which grossed millions. His sudden death on 20 July 1973, at the age of just thirty-two, sent the media into a frenzy of speculation about conspiracy theories: a mysterious martial arts sect had been hostile to Lee for divulging *kung-fu* secrets to the West; Triads, the Chinese Mafia, had killed him for refusing to pay protection money ...

Officially, Lee died from an acute reaction to aspirin. On the last day of his life, he had been at the film studio, working through the script of his latest movie with his leading lady, Betyy Ting-pei, when he complained of a headache and took a break. Several hours later attempts to wake him failed and he was rushed to the hospital.

The coincidence in this anecdote came about when almost twenty years later (31 March 1993), Lee's son Brandon, also an actor, became ill on the set of a movie and died suddenly reviving once again the bizarre stories about Lee's surprise death.

46. Hitler and Stalin

School class photographs of the young Hitler and the young Stalin bear striking resemblances. The photos were taken when each was about ten, Stalin's in 1889 and Hitler's in 1899. They appear in the centre of the back row of their classes. Each is wearing a distinctive look of defiant superiority that somehow demands attention.

The coincidences do not end there, according to Lord Bullock, author of *Hitler and Stalin Parallel Lives* (1991).

Bullock points out both men had bullying fathers and doting mothers. Both were short men, the German dictator, 167.6 centimetres and the Russian dictator, 162.5 centimetres. Both were misogynists who had female lovers who shot themselves. Neither had much interest in sex. Both were seriously underestimated by their political rivals, who dismissed them as boorish little men. Psychologically, they were narcissistic. Neither

could stand the slightest criticism. They were revenge-obsessed, nocturnal, anti-semitic and unpredictable.

Bullock goes into detail of how both men mastered the arts of revolutionary politics; how they were geniuses, their timing superb. They were congenitally deceitful and had an instinctive understanding of where power lay. They claimed ultimate power over their separate nations in the same year, 1934.

47. Story of a Coincidence

On May 5, 1974, *The Sunday Times* of London published the results of a competition for the best story of a coincidence. Among more than 2,000 letters submitted was the following from Mr. D. J. Page, of Surrey, England:

In the month of July, 1940, I was a young soldier in the service of His Majesty at the time somewhere in England. I was to discover that my long- awaited wedding photographs had been opened mistakenly by a soldier in another Troop (A), my Troop being "B." He was apologetic, having opened the letter, and realised his error, which was not surprising, seeing that our names and numbers were so similar. His name being Pape, No. 1509322 and my name being Pape, No. 1509321. This mix up in the mail being frequent until I was posted to another Battery. Sometime after the war had ended, I was employed as a driver with London Transport at the Merton depot, Colliers Wood, S.W. London.

One particular pay day, I'd noticed that the tax deduction was very heavy, and duly presented myself to the superintendent's office. . . . Imagine my amazement when I discovered that my wages had been mixed up with a driver who had been transferred to the garage, not so surprising when I found out that his name was Pape, yes, the very same chap. . . . The weirdest thing of all, our P.S.V. License Nos. were-mine–29222, Mr. Pape's 29223.

48. The Prophetic Photograph

Mrs. Eileen M. Bithell of Portsmouth, England, tells the following story of a long-hidden but prophetic photograph:

For over twenty years, there hung in the window of my parents' grocery shop a framed sign which stated one day of the week on which the shop was closed. Two weeks before my brother's wedding, the sign was taken down to be altered and was removed from its frame.

Behind the sign was found a large photograph showing a small girl held in her father's arms. The small girl was my brother's bride-to-be and the man, his future father-in-law. No one knows how this particular photograph came to be used as a backing for the shop sign as none of the people in the photograph was then known to my family, yet now, twenty years later, the two families were to be joined by marriage.

49. Pele Scores Ten

Pele, one of the world's most famous soccer players, was obsessed with the number 10. Playing for Brazil, he drew the number 10 jersey both times he played for that country's successful World Cup winning teams. When touring, he stayed in room number 10 on the tenth floor and made sure the number plate of one of his cars added up to 10.

50. Taxi Number

Colin Archer drove a cab for fifteen years with the numberplate T 390. His private car numberplate was CRA 390, and when he wrote away for a ticket for a senior citizens' week concert, he was sent a ticket numbered 390. The following year when he received his ticket to the concert, it was again 390.

51. Chewing Bait

Andrew White, thirteen, was fishing with his family on Smiths Lake in Australia one day in January 1994 and dropped his green-coloured chewing gum overboard when it lost its taste. Within minutes, his brother Greg caught a fish and when it was gutted back on shore, they found inside the discarded wad of chewing gum.

52. Heart to Heart

John and Arthur Mowforth were twins. "What happened to one," their sister said, "usually happened to the other". On the evening of May 22, 1975, each experienced severe chest pain and was rushed (unbeknown to the other or their families) to the hospital—one in Bristol and the other in Windsor, 110 or 125 kms away as the crow flies. Each man died of a heart attack, shortly after arrival.

53. Rejection Manuscript

On a Friday night, early in 1992, a London publisher was dining in a Notting Hill Gate restaurant when thieves broke into her car. Among the things stolen was a manuscript she had big hopes for, although she had not yet told its author. Its loss was what most upset her about the incident.

The thieves, however, obviously didn't think highly of the manuscript and had thrown it over a wall before driving away.

She spent a nervous weekend and in her office on Monday morning was trying to decide how she should deal with the problem when a call came from the author of the manuscript. In a voice tinged more with sorrow than anger, he asked the publisher: "Why did you have my manuscript thrown over my front fence?"

54. The Unfortunate Anagram

Sir Peter Scott, one of Britain's best-known naturalists, is an enthusiastic believer in the Loch Ness monster and has lent the weight of his reputation to the debate about it for many years. So great, in fact, is his confidence in the creature's existence that he has promoted the use of a Greek name for it: *Nessiteras rhombopteryx.* This name, which he and underwater photographer Robert L. Rines coined in December 1975, may be roughly translated as "The Ness monster with diamond-shaped fin." As London newspapers quickly

pointed out with some glee, the name is also an anagram for the words, "Monster Hoax by Sir Peter S."

55. A Shared Fate

A man riding a moped was killed by a taxi in Bermuda in 1975, exactly a year after his brother had been killed—on the same street, by the same taxi driver carrying the same passenger, and on the same moped.

56. A Day for Politics

On 19th December 1991, Paul Keating took over from Bob Hawke as Australian Prime Minister. On 19th December 1931, the Labour Party, led by James Scullin, lost government in a landslide to the Conservatives. On 19th December 1949, Sir Robert Menzies was sworn in as Prime Minister. On 19th December 1967, John "Black Jack" McEwen was sworn in as temporary Prime Minister. On 19th December, again in 1972, the first Labour government since 1949 was sworn in. In 1992, Mr Keating came within a whisker of calling a snap 19th December poll.

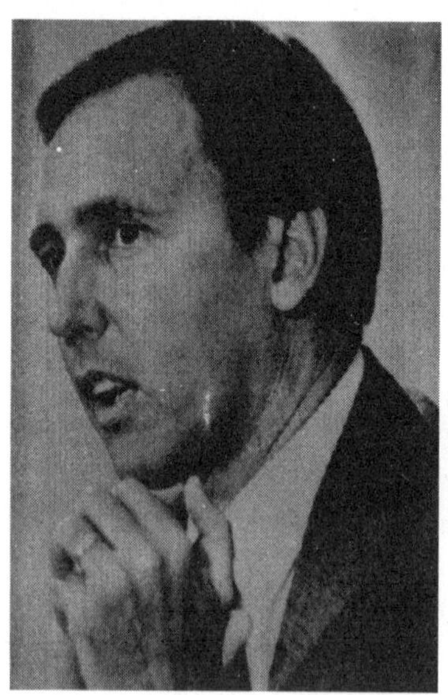

The circumstances leading up to these six significant events so widely separated in time were all unrelated and the date had no other significance in Australia.

57. The Escaped Spy

At the beginning of World War I, French intelligence agents arrested a German spy, Peter Karpin, as soon as he entered the country. They kept the arrest secret, however, and for the next three years, until Karpin's escape in 1917, sent fake reports to his superiors and intercepted all funds sent to France on his behalf. These funds were used to buy an automobile, which, in 1919, ran down and killed a man in the Ruhr, at that time still occupied by the French. The victim of the accident was none other than the escaped spy, Peter Karpin.

58. Bookmark

During World War II, Yorkshireman, Arthur Butterworth was stationed at an army camp on the grounds of Taversham Hall, near Norwich. He had ordered a secondhand book on music from a London bookseller, and when the parcel eventually arrived, he opened it in his hut, standing at his window. As he did so, a picture postcard fell out of the book, evidently placed there as a bookmark by the previous owner. Butterworth saw that the card had been written on August 4, 1913, and he turned it over to look at the picture. To his astonishment, the photograph showed exactly what he could see from his window-Taversham Hall.

Since army camps during the war were signified solely by a postcode, and to by name, the bookseller could not have known where he was sending the parcel and therefore, could not deliberately have included the card as a friendly gesture. In a book about music, Arthur Butterworth found not an ordinary gift but a baffling resonance of time and space.

59. Assemblage in Paris

When the novelist, Anne Parrish first visited Paris in the 1920's, she and her husband spent sometime browsing among the secondhand bookstalls that line the banks of the River Seine near the Ile de la Cite. In one stall, she found an old copy of *Jack Frost and Other Stories*, a book she had loved as a small child in Colorado Springs and had not seen since her nursery days. Excited to meet such an old friend again after so many years, she showed the book to her husband. He opened it and on the flyleaf found an inscription: "Anne Parrish, 209 N. Weber Street, Clorado Springs.".

60. False Prescription

In early March 1987, constable Douglas McKenzie was sent with his partner, constable Gary Tomas, to arrest a man being held in a central Sydney chemist's shop for using false prescriptions. At the shop, constable McKenzie asked the accused man to identify himself. 'Douglas McKenzie,' said the man, who produced a birth certificate, university card, two bankbooks and a health care card, all in the name of McKenzie.

'I said to him, you can't be Douglas McKenzie - because that's me,' McKenzie recalled.

The identifying items had disappeared from the constable's car about two years before, while it was parked in Sydney's night-life district, King's Cross, a haunt of criminals, addicts and pushers, prostitutes and pimps.

'When I said the items were mine, he knew he was gone,' said constable McKenzie. His face went stone cold and his jaw almost hit the ground. Finding someone who has taken over your identity leaves you with a pretty strange feeling. It's the strangest arrest I have ever made." At the time of the incident, the constable had been stationed in Central police station, the busiest in New South Wales, with hundreds of police on duty at any one time.

61. Another Plane Story

This case concerns a small-world story involving actor Gordon Chater. He was flying from London to New York after a twenty-week tour as one of the leading actors in the play, *The Dresser.*

On Concorde Chater chatted with the woman sitting next to him, who said it was her fist trip to New York. 'And why are you going?' asked the actor. 'Well,' she replied 'my husband is Ronald Hardwood, and he has written a play that you probably haven't heard of. It's called *The Dresser* and it's opening in New York . . .'

62. The 11-Digit Number

The following story appeared in *The Washington Post* for April 20, 1978:

Wanda Marie Johnson, of Adelphi, Maryland, Prince Georges County, is a baggage clerk at Union Station in Washington.

Wanda Marie Johnson, of Suitland, Maryland, Prince Georges County, is a nurse at D.C. General Hospital in Washington.

Both Wanda Maries were born on the same day, June 15, 1953; both moved from Washington, D.C., to Prince Georges County, both had two children, delivered in the same hospital, and both owned two-door Ford Granadas: the 11-digits serial numbers on their cars were the same except for the last three digits.

63. Identical Twin Boys

Identical twin boys, born in Ohio, some 40 years ago, were adopted by different families shortly after their birth. In 1979, after 39 years apart, they were reunited. It was discovered that

each had been named James; each had had law-enforcement training; each liked mechanical drawing and carpentry. Each married woman named Linda, had a son — one named James Alan and the other James Allan-had divorced, and then married a second wife, named Betty. Both had had dogs named Toy. Also, both favoured the same St. Petersburg, Florida vacation beach.

64. Eighteen, Eighteen ....

Henry Longfellow (1807-82) wrote eighteen volumes of poetry, graduated from Bowdoin College at eighteen, married his second wife, eighteen years later, was a professor at Harvard for eighteen years and died on the 18th of March.

65. Allah is Great

Sophy Burnham, author of the best-seller, *A Book of Angels*, relates in an HQ magazine interview how, in her research for a four-line quote from the Koran, one afternoon, on a sudden whim, she wandered into a bookshop, sure that she would find the quote there. As she picked up a copy of the Koran, she suddenly realised just how huge the book is. Also, she had no idea where the quote was; she could have been searching forever to find it. So she offered up a brief prayer, then allowed the book to fall open - and looked down. On the page before her was the four-line quote.

66. Same Titles

Journalist Peter Watson went undercover for a book he wrote that resulted in this coincidence. He posed as an art dealer called John Blake in order to recover a stolen Caravaggio painting. The book of his experiences he called, *The Caravaggio Conspiracy.* In the week it was published, a novel by Oliver Banks also came out, called *The Caravaggio Obsession*, a fictional account of an art dealer trying to locate a stolen Caravaggio. In it, the fictional dealer's name is Richard Blake. Watson had had some dealings with coincidences before this: He had written a book about the coincidences in the lives of identical twins.

67. Swiss Twirl

To add to the notion of the literary 'universal mind' as opposed to the mind-set of the plagiarist, Sir Arthur Conan Doyle tells of a literary coincidence in his *Through the Magic Door* (Doyle, famed for his creation of the character, Sherlock Holmes, was also a spiritualist). He was staying in Switzerland and had visited the Gemini Pass, where a high cliff separates French from the

German cantons. On the summit of the cliff was a small inn which used to be isolated in winter for three months as it became inaccessible during heavy snowfall. His imagination was stirred and he began to build a short story of strong antagonistic characters being stuck at the inn, loathing each other yet utterly unable to get away from each other's company, each day bringing them nearer to tragedy . . .

On his way back to Britain, in France, he came across a volume of Maupassant's Tales. The first story was called "L'Aubege". The scene was set in the very inn he had visited and the plot was the same as he had imagined, except that Maupassant brought in a savage hound. Doyle's initial reaction was relief that he had avoided a charge of plagiarism. He believed the coincidence was spiritually inspired, and was a psychic coincidence.

68. Iraqi Nuclear Reactor

Robert Hutchenson had been working for two years on a fictional story about the Israelis attacking an Iraqi nuclear reactor. In 1981, while he was still completing the novel, it actually happened.

69. One Big Coincidence

On November 22, 1941, 16 days before the Japanese attack on Pearl Harbour—*The New Yorker* ran two advertisements for a new dice game called The Deadly Double. One of the advertisements carried the headline ACHTUNG. WARNING. ALERTE! At the foot of the column were the words, THE DEADLY DOUBLE, and beneath the words a double-headed heraldic eagle (in the manner of the armorial device of Germany) with a shield on its breast bearing a double cross. The other advertisement showed two dice, on black and the other white, each with three visible faces. On the faces of the white dice were the number, 12 and 24 and the double-cross sign: On the black dice were the number, 0, 5, and 7. Above the dice the headline words, ACHTUNG. WARNNING. ALERTE! were repeated.

After the Pearl Harbour attack, there was much speculation that the advertisements had been placed by the Axis powers to alert their agents: The numbers 12 and 7 could have referred to the date of the attack (December 7), the numbers 5 and 0 could have indicated the planned time of the attack, and XX (20 in Roman numerals) might have stood for the approximate latitude of the target; and the significance of the 24 was unknown. So strong were these suspicions that FBI agents visited the people who had placed the advertisements, Mr. and Mrs. Roger Craig.

The game of Deadly Double was legitimate and was being sold by several New York department stores in 1941. The government's suspicions were kept quiet until 1967 when Ladislas Farago, formerly with U.S. naval intelligence, revealed the story in the press release for his book, *The Broken Seal.* Interviewed by a reporter shortly after, Roger Craig's widow said that any connection between the advertisements and Pearl Harbour "was just one big coincidence."

70. They Survived

The police sergeant, Ron King reports that on 10th June 1982, he had a serious accident at 1.30 a.m., driving a Toyota Corolla. He received many broken ribs and was left with a large scar under his chin.

On 10th June 1984, ('yep, at 1.30 a.m. exactly') his son, Peter, was also involved in an accident while driving a Toyota Corolla. He had no broken bones, but was left with a scar under his chin.

The coincidence did not end there. His daughter fell over late 1986. Now she ,too, bears a scar under her chin. They are all grateful, they survived to tell the story.

71. Unfortunate Coincidence

In October 1979, Anthony William O'Sullivan escaped from jail and managed to elude capture for many months.

One day in April, the following year, he rang a house and was arrested shortly afterwards. He had made the call at the time the police were searching it for drugs. The police answered the phone and asked some pertinent questions, such as, where he was at that moment, without O'Sullivan being aware that he was speaking to the police.

72. As Carl Jung Told

Carl Jung told of a German mother who photographed her infant son in 1914. She left the one-shot film plate to be developed at Strasbourg, but the outbreak of the First World War prevented her from returning to Strasbourg.

Two years later, she bought a film plate from Frankfurt, more than 160 kilometres away. She used it to take a picture of her daughter. When that plate was developed, superimposed on the picture was the earlier picture of her son. The plate had somehow been labelled unused and sent to Frankfurt, then sold to her. With cases like that being reported to him, no wonder Jung remained fascinated.

73. Difference Between Mysticism

Dr. Lawrence LeShan, a psychologist who has written extensively on meditation and paranormal phenomena, published the following letter in the *international Journal of Parapsychology* in 1968:

In the very first days of December, 1967, I sent the draft of a manuscript dealing largely with mysticism to the well-known psychologist, Dr. Nina Ridenour. Although she is best known for her professional work in mental health, Dr. Ridenour is also an expert on mysticism.

At noon of December 11, Dr. Ridenour and I met for lunch to discuss my paper. I was taking notes of her comments and criticisms throughout the discussion. Her central argument was that my manuscript reflected my less than perfect knowledge of mysticism. When she suggested a number of books on the subject I should read, I took down the entire list. She mentioned eight works, books by Nicoll, Stance and Ouspensky among them. The fifth book, Dr. Ridenour mentioned was Byng's, *The Vision of Asia.* To my clear recollection, she said, after I had written down both the author's name and the title: "Until you read this, you won't understand the difference between eastern and western mysticism." Although I did not record this particular comment of her, I can still hear her voice saying precisely these words, and my notes contain the reference with a check mark after it.

Dr. Ridenour's comment had impressed me, for the differences between Eastern and Western mysticism are crucial to the idea, I have been trying to explore. Consequently, I went out straight from luncheon meeting to the library of the Parapsychology Foundation to see whether they had this book, but they did not. From the Foundation, I went directly to the library of Union Theological Seminary to find the book, again without success.

That evening, on my way home, I was in a hurry as I was late. Yet on sheer impulse I took a route I had never taken before, because it is about 50 paces longer. Pausing for a moment at a traffic light next to a rash basket, I saw a book lying on the ground. Prompted by idle curiosity, I bent down and picked it up. The volume I held in my hand was entitled, *The Vision of Asia,* and the author's name was L. A. Cranmer-Byng.

The next morning I called Dr. Ridenour and said: "I have a funny story to tell you about the book you recommended." She replied, " Which book? I said, "*The Vision of Asia* by Byng." "I never heard of it, " she answered.

And there, as Kipling would put it, the matter rests. Dr. Ridenour, who is a serious and highly responsible person, is quite clear about the fact of the book until I mentioned it to her. I have the book (a library copy removed from the Columbia University oriental Library in 1960) and my notes taken as she was talking, including the reference to the book.

I must say that I am unable to classify this experience into any general category.

74. The Girl From Petrovka

When early in the 1970's the British actor, Anthony Hopkins signed a contract to play one of the leading roles in a film version of George Feifer's, *The girl From Petrovka,* he scoured the bookshops in London's Charing Cross Road for a copy of the original novel. His search was in vain, and in some frustration he went into the Leicester Square subway station to catch a train home. And there, lying on a bench in the station, he found a copy of the book, apparently forgotten by some fellow traveller.

Two years later, Hopkins was in Vienna, working on the film production, and was visited by George Feifer. Feifer told him that he had no copy of his own book — he had given his last one to a friend who had lost it in London. " Is this the one, "Hopkins asked, handing him the book, "with the notes scribbled in the margins?" It was, indeed, Feifer's own copy. The girl from Petrovka had come home at last.

75. Familiar Eyes !

In 1983, sisters, Pat Speer and Madelaine Cook were reunited after eighteen years when they bumped into each other at a supermarket checkout in San Francisco. 'I saw her look at me,' Pat said. 'I did a doubletake. I thought, "My god, those eyes are familiar!" Then I asked her if she was Mickey and she said, "Are you Patti?"'

They had not seen one another since Pat had run away from her adoptive parents at the age of sixteen. The sisters shortly afterwards found their natural mother — and a brother.

76. Lightning Knocked Twice

Boston councillor Albert O'Neill, speaking in 1984 on radio, vowed he would look into the abortion controversy. 'May lightning strike me dead if I don't,' he declared. At that moment a lightning bolt knocked the station off the air. Nobody was hurt.

In 1988, lightning struck the Sydney Radio 2KY transmitter and put the station off the air as racing commentator Chris Kearns was discussing the chances of a greyhound called Silence.

77. Revenue Relationship

Two women in US were brought together by the taxation office — the Internal Revenue Service — in a meeting full of coincidence. In 1983, the IRS told Mrs Patricia Kern that she owed $3,000 in tax for a job she held in Oregon. Mrs Kern wrote back and said she had never been to Oregon. The service finally traced a Patricia Dibiasi, who lived in Oregon and who did owe the taxes.

As a result, the following facts emerged. The two women shared the same maiden name, birthday and social security number. Both were born on 31st March, 1942 and were renamed Patricia Ann Campbell. Their fathers were named Robert. They both had worked as book-keepers and studied cosmetics. The ages of their children were the same. Their husbands were servicemen. Both were married within eleven days of each other in 1959. Finally, they had never met.

78. A Case of Kimono

A kimono, successively owned by three teenage girls, each of them died before she had a chance to wear it, was believed to be so unlucky that it was cremated by a Japanese priest in February 1657. As the garment was being burned, a violent wind sprang up, fanning the flames and spreading them beyond control. The ensuing fire destroyed three-quarters of Tokyo, levelling 300 temples, 500 places, 9,000 shops, 61 bridges, and killing 100,000 people.

79. Double Exposure

Jabez Spicer, of Leyden, Massachusetts, was killed by two bullets in the attack on the federal arsenal at Springfield on January 25, 1787, during Shays's Rebellion. At the time, he was wearing the same coat his brother Daniel had been wearing when he, too, was killed by two bullets on March 5, 1784.

The bullets that killed Jabez Spicer passed through the holes made by the bullets that had killed his brother Daniel, three years earlier.

80. Clocking Out

An ornate clock belonging to King Louis XIV of France stopped at the precise moment of his death, 7:45 a.m., on September 1, 1715, and has never run since.

81. Political Kidnapping

A book foretold the kidnapping and brainwashing of American heiress Patty Hearst. The novel, *Black Abductor* by James Rusk, was published in 1973 and related the events of 1974 with stunning accuracy. Both the kidnapping and the novel share the following features. A young college student named Patricia, daughter of a wealthy and prominent right-wing figure, is kidnapped near her university campus while she is with her boyfriend, who is severely beaten. Initially, the boyfriend is a suspect in the case. The kidnappers, led by an angry young black man, are members of a terrorist revolutionary group. At first, the girl is an unwilling captive but later, she adopts their ideology and joins the group. In what is termed 'America's first political kidnapping, the group sent Polaroid pictures of the young woman, along with messages to her father.

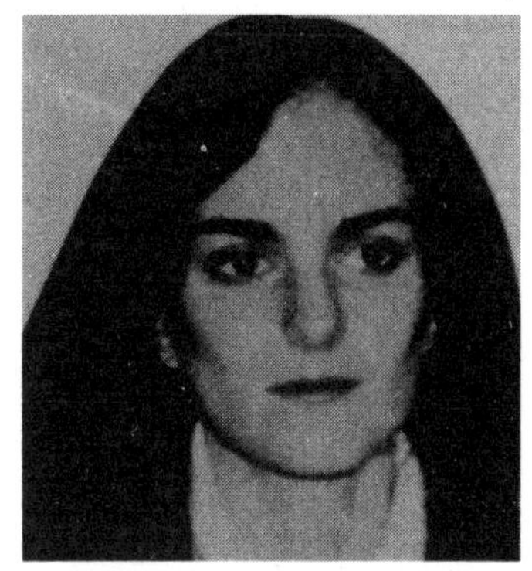

The fictional abductors predict — as happened in the real abduction — that they will ultimately be surrounded by the police, tear-gassed and killed.

Four weeks after the Hearst kidnapping, the FBI visited author Rusk. They suspected that either he was involved in the planning and kidnapping or that the kidnapper had got the idea from his book. They had difficulty in accepting it for the coincidence it was.

82. 1942 Penny

Barbara Mercier, who turned fifty late in 1991, was given a 1942 penny by her brother to make the occasion. She placed the penny on top of the family video.

The following day, Mrs Mercier took her young granddaughter, Cassie, to the doctor's. In the waiting room, she noticed the child playing with a 1942 penny and admonished her for taking it from the video. Cassie insisted she had not, she had found the coin there in the waiting room.

When they returned home, the other 1942-penny was still sitting on top of the video.

83. The Unfailing Pistol

The following story is told by Sir Harold Nicolson in his essay, "Coincidences:"

In May of 1866, Prince Bismark, while riding on the Unter Den Linden, was approached by a student named Cohen Blind, who pulled out a revolver and fired four shots at point-blank range. Two of the bullets missed their mark, one entered Bismark's shoulder, and one penetrated the lung. The Iron Chancellor was not a man to be disturbed by a little thing like that, and in six days, he could again be observed, erect and dominant, riding

down the Unter den Linden. Herr Blind, meanwhile, had been arrested and the revolver had been taken from him. It was presented to Bismark as a souvenir of the occasion.

In 1886, the father of my friend, Leopold was staying with Bismark, to whom he was related by marriage. There were several ladies staying in the house, and after luncheon, the Princess Bismark took the ladies around the rooms, showing them the historical objects which they contained. Bismark himself and the men guests remained in the smoking-room puffing Hamburg cigars. The voices of the ladies could be heard in the Chancellor's study. "And this," a voice said, "is the pistol which Blind used in 1866." There was a murmur of interest followed by a loud report. Bismark leapt from his chair and dashed into the adjoining room: The ladies were standing looking at each other in astonishment: a smell of powder hung in the air. The pistol, still smoking, lay upon the ground. The Chancellor gave way to one of his rare outburst of fury. How could, he thundered, anyone have been so foolish as to touch the revolver? It was a mere miracle that no one had been killed. Never must anyone be allowed to touch that weapon again.

In 1906, my friend Leopold was also staying with his cousins at Friedrichsruh. It was a wet afternoon, and some young people had come over to luncheon. He showed them the Chancellor's study. He took up the pistol from the writing table. "This," he said, "is the pistol with which Blind shot at Bismark in 1866. Twenty years later, when my father was staying here, some ladies were visiting the house and one of them took up the pistol and foolishly pulled the trigger like this . . . " there was a flash and report. They leapt aside and stared at each other with white faces. One of the girls had been slightly hurt in the hand: Leopold himself was bleeding at the finger, and his hand was burnt and black with gunpowder. The bullet, the sixth and last bullet in the revolver of Herr Blind, was imbedded in his biceps.

84. Different Reasons

Life magazine carried a story which told how all fifteen people who were to attend the choir practice in Beatrice, Nebraska, due to start at 7.15 p.m. on the 1st of March 1950, were late. Each had a different reason: A car would not start, a radio programme was not over, ironing wasn't finished, a conversation dragged on, etc. The church was destroyed by an explosion at 7.25 p.m. The chances of their being late were later estimated at one in a million. The choir members did not attribute their lateness to probability but to a more obvious source.

85. Bullet that Killed

In 1883, Henry Ziegland, of Honey Grove, Texas, jilted his sweetheart, who then killed herself. Her brother tried to avenge her by shooting Ziegland, but the bullet only grazed his face and buried itself in a tree. The brother, believing that he killed Ziegland, then took his own life.

In 1913, Ziegland was cutting down the tree with the bullet in it. It was a difficult job, so he used dynamite. The explosion sent the old bullet through Ziegland's head and killed him.

86. Reburial of an Actor

Canadian actor Charles Coghlan became ill and died in Galveston, Texas, during a tour of the American State in 1899. He was buried in a lead coffin which was sealed inside a vault.

In September 1900, less than a year after his burial, a hurricane hit Galveston, flooding the cemetery and breaking open the vault. Coghlan's coffin floated away, into the Gulf of Mexico, then drifted along the Florida coastline and into the Atlantic, where the Gulf stream took over and carried it north.

One day in 1908, some fishermen on Prince Edward Island, Canada, saw a long, weather-beaten box floating ashore — Coghlan's coffin. The actor's body had floated more than 5,600 kilometres to his home. His fellow islanders reburied him in the graveyard of the church where he had been baptised.

87. A Couple from Leningrad

Geoff Kenihan and his wife, travel-writer Kerry, entered the Hotel Leningrad dining room by one door as an elderly couple, Roger and Alice, entered from another on 2nd August, 1971. Both the couples zeroed in on an empty table in the room and ended up sharing it. They enjoyed the meal and one another's company, and departed never expecting to meet again.

On 2nd August, 1972 (note the date), Geoff and Kerry entered the Indian restaurant of the Hotel Oberoi in Singapore and headed for the one empty table as another couple, who had simultaneously entered through another door, were doing the same — Roger and Alice from Leningrad.

88. Death 157 Years Apart

In January 1889, Elizabeth Bromfield was walking home from the church along the Adelaide Street, in the New South Wales town of Blayney, when lightning killed her.

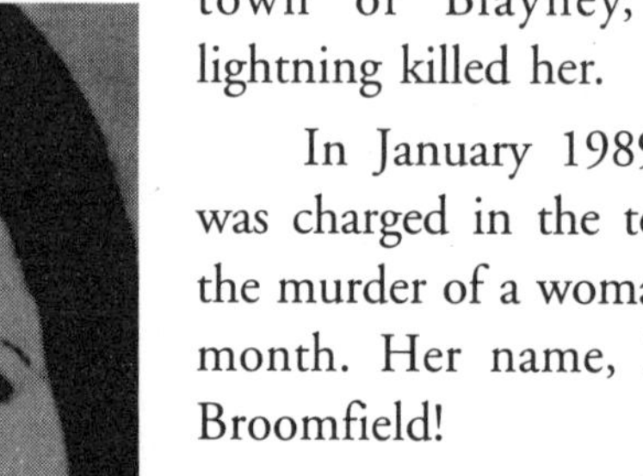

In January 1989, a man was charged in the town with the murder of a woman in that month. Her name, Elizabeth Broomfield!

Now there is a strange similar story. Two girls of the same age were murdered on the same day and in the same place, 157 years apart. The details:

On 27th May, 1817, Mary Ashford, twenty, was found dead at Erdington, then a village about eight kilometres from Birmingham. On 27th May, 1974, the strangled body of Barbara Forrest, twenty, was found at Erdington, by then a suburb of Birmingham.

Forrest's body was found in long grass near the Erdington children's home where she worked as a nurse, about 350 metres from the spot where Ashford's body had been dumped. And 26th May in both 1817 and 1974 was not only a Monday but a Whit-Monday.

The pattern of the girls' movements just before their deaths was similar. Both had visited a friend earlier in the evening where they had (both) changed their dress to go on to a dance. Both women had been raped before being murdered. They had died at about the same time.

The man arrested for each murder was named Thornton! Both were acquitted. So both cases remain unsolved.

89. Experts Fooled

Eighteen senior Health Department bureaucrats attended a conference dinner early in 1992 — and were all struck down with food poisoning!

90. Fiery Stories

In the California fires of 1993, British film director Duncan Gibbins died from burns while trying to rescue his Siamese cat. Gibbins had credits for three hit movies. He co-wrote the *Third Degree Burns* (1989) directed *Fire with Fire* (1986) and co-wrote and directed *Eve of Destruction* (1991). As their titles suggest, all had to do with fire and destruction.

The cat was later found safe but singed.

91. Cannonball Curse

Keith Pritchard, thirty-one, an accredited racing-car driver and official in the world's first legal Cannonball Run, was a worried man, a few days before the event in early 1994.

He told his parents that Japanese entrant Akihiro Kabe, a millionaire dentist from Tokyo, was absolutely crazy and was going to kill somebody, according to Pritchard's mother.

As he was coming into a checkpoint, 150 kms south of Alice Springs, Kabe's Ferrari spun out of control and crashed into an official car, killing himself and three others, including the man who had predicted tragedy, Keith Pritchard.

92. The Golden Matchbox

When King Edward VII of England was a young man, and still the prince of Wales, he was a keen fox hunter. One of his frequent companions in the hunt was an actor named Edward A. Sothern. One day, as a mark of esteem and affection, the prince gave his friend a golden matchbox designed to be attached to a watch chain. Sothern carried the matchbox with him wherever he went, but one day, when he was out hunting he was thrown from his horse, and the box, despite all efforts to find it, was lost. Sothern had a duplicate made and later gave it to his son Lytton as a present.

Lytton Sothern was also an actor, and during a tour of Australia, he gave the duplicate matchbox to a friend there named Labertouche.

Back in England, Lytton's brother George, a fox hunter like his father, was riding one day when he came upon the old farmer whose land the hunt was using. Learning that George was the son of Edward A. Sothern, the farmer presented him with the golden box lost 20 years earlier and found only that morning by a farmhand who had been out ploughing.

Lytton and George's brother, Edward H. Sothern — the third actor in the family — was on tour in America when this incident occurred, and George found the incident striking enough to write to him about it. When Edward read the letter, he was travelling by train with another actor, Arthur Lawrence, whom he had met for the first time that day. He told Lawrence the curious story and wondered what had become of the duplicate box. Whereupon, to his astonishment, Lawrence dangled a chain in front of him. On it was the golden matchbox given to Lawrence by Mr. Labertouche.

93. Emperor Franz of Austria

In 1849, Emperor Franz Josef of Austria, then nineteen, was visited by an obscure Hungarian countess who accused him of having had her son murdered. Young Michael Karoli had been executed on the orders of Baron Julius von Haynau, general of Franz Josef's army, as he tried to put down the Hungarian revolt against the empire.

Countess Karoli followed her accusation with a five-part curse: 'May heaven and hell blast your happiness. May your family be exterminated. May you be smitten through the persons of those you love. May your life be wrecked. May your children be brought to ruin.'

The curse was to be appallingly fulfilled. More than a dozen of his close relatives met violent deaths. Other abdicated, were compromised in scandals or involved in bad marriages.

Franz Josef married a sixteen-year-old Elisabeth, with whom he was smitten, but they remained faithful for only a few weeks before she found another lover and the emperor also sought consolation outside the marriage.

He soon had other problems. Austria fought a war against France, Sardinia and Prussia and lost every battle. His empire shrank and Austria was driven from the German Confederation. In 1867, his wife's brother-in-law, Maximilian was rejected as Emperor of Mexico and shot by a firing squad.

From 1886, his wife's cousin, mad King Ludwig of Bavaria, committed suicide by drowning, his niece, Sophie was burnt to death and his son, Crown Prince Rudolph took his own life. His nephew, John of Saxony abdicated and was then drowned at sea, while another nephew, Archduke William, died in a fall from a horse. Another niece was burnt to death and three more nephews committed suicide. In 1897, the Empress Elisabeth was murdered by an Italian in Geneva.

In 1941, his heir, Archduke Ferdinand, was assassinated in Sarajevo triggering the First World War. Franz Josef died a lonely, exhausted figure as the Allies crushed his army in 1916.

94. Shipping Disaster

Talking of storms ... Australia's worst shipping disaster occurred on 4th August, 1845, when a hurricane drove the *Catarqui* on to a reef, 500 metres off King Island in Bass Strait.

The 802-tonne migrant ship had sailed from Liverpool, four months earlier with 415 men, women and children on board. Only nine made it to the shore, including the first mate, Thomas Guthrie, and the only migrant to survive was Sol Brown, whose wife and four children were among those drowned.

Guthrie took a job as skipper of a coastal vessel and was drowned a year later when his ship went aground off South Australia. Three years after the tragedy, Brown fell into a creek late one night when drunk and he, too, finally drowned in a few inches of water.

95. Coincidence at Sea

One of the most amazing coincidences at sea began innocently enough, with the departure from Sydney Harbour on 16th October, 1829 of the schooner *Mermaid*, bound for distant Collier Bay on the north-west coast of Western Australia, thousands of kilometres away. On board were eighteen crew and three passengers. The captain was Samuel Nolbrow.

The journey along the east coast of the country went smoothly for four days. Then a sudden gale blew up as the *Mermaid* was entering the Torres Strait, between Australia's northern tip and Papua New Guinea. High winds and raging seas tossed the helpless schooner in every direction. Finally, a large wave dumped her on a reef and she began to break up. The only chance for those on board was to swim to a rocky peak that jutted from the boiling waters, about 100 metres from where they had gone down.

At daybreak, a head count showed that all those on board had somehow made it through the raging sea. They were marooned there, cold and wet, for three days before another ship, the barque *Swiftsure*, appeared.

The *Swiftsure* took the survivors on board and continued on her way, heading west for five days along the southern coast of Papua New Guinea. Unexpectedly, she found herself under the influence of a strong current. Her crew unable to counter it, the ship was swept on to rocks and wrecked. The *Mermaid's* crew found themselves abandoning the ship for the second time.

This time the ordeal lasted only eight hours. The schooner *Governor Ready* spotted their signals from the shore. The *Governor Ready* was already carrying thirty-two people and a full cargo of timber. However, she managed to squeeze the survivors from both the *Mermaid* and *Swiftsure* on board before continuing her voyage.

Only three hours later, the *Governor* mysteriously caught fire. The fire spread rapidly through the timber and the order to abandon ship yet again rang out. Everybody jammed into her long boats. Around them was nothing but a vast expanse of open sea and their prospects of yet another rescue looked slim. But a miracle occurred. The government cutter *Comet* unexpectedly appeared, and again all were rescued.

When the story so far spread among the crew of the *Comet*, there was some initial grumbling about the *Mermaid's* crew being jinxed. But it was pointed out that rather than a bad luck they were having a great deal of good luck. So far they had survived three shipwrecks in dangerous waters.

For a week, the good luck argument prevailed — until another sudden squall sprang up. Soon the *Comet's* mast was lost, her sails in tatters, her rudder gone. This time the only ones to abandon the ship were the crew of the *Comet*. Their belief in the jinx theory by this time prevailed and they took to their boats, leaving their shipwrecked fellow seafarers to fend for themselves.

For eighteen hours those left behind on the *Comet* clung to what was little more than a wreck. They had to fight off sharks as well as weariness throughout their ordeal. They were saved yet again when the packet *Jupiter* appeared and took all on board.

As they, at last, headed for port, the captains took the roll and realised that, although there had been four shipwrecks, not a single life had been lost.

An incredible story on its own! However, there was a final coincidence. On board the last vessel – *Jupiter* - was a passenger, Sarah Richey, an elderly Yorkshire woman. She was in Australia searching for her son, Peter, who had been missing for fifteen years. Peter was one of the crew from the first vessel, *Mermaid.*

96. The Plum Pudding

Plum puddings are an English rather than a French speciality, and the French poet Émile Deschamps, who as a child at a boarding school in Orleans, around 1800, had been urged to try a slice by a M. de Fortgibu (who had just returned from England) — remembered the dessert very well.

Ten years later, Deschamps was passing by a restaurant in Paris when he noticed inside it a plum pudding of fine appearance. He went in to order a slice but was told that another customer had already ordered for the pudding. "Monsieur de Fortgibu," the lady at the counter called out to an approaching customer, "would you have goodness to share your plum pudding with this gentleman?" Deschamps's old plum pudding benefactor was now an elderly man with powdered hair and wearing the uniform of a colonel.

He was more than willing to share his pudding again with Deschamps. Greeting each other, the two men reminisced about the earlier plum pudding.

Many years went by, and Deschamps found himself invited to a dinner party at which, he was told, plum pudding would be served. "Then I know M. De Fortgibu will be there," Deschamps told his hostess and amused her with the story.

The evening of the dinner party arrived, and at the conclusion of the meal, a magnificent plum pudding was served to the 10 guests. At that very moment, the door opened and in wandered, M. de Fortgibu. By now very old, and somewhat disoriented, he had mistaken the address, he was aiming for and had arrived at the party by error.

97. The Relevant Papyrus

The Angel of Libraries, whose task is to look after deserving authors and scholars, is perhaps an Egyptologist at heart, for one of her choicest gifts of coincidence was bestowed on Dr. Thomas Young, the English physicist who, with Jean Francis Champollion, was largely responsible for deciphering the Rosetta stone, the first and major key to our understanding of hieroglyphics.

One evening in 1822 (the year in which Champollion, taking his cue from Young's research, published his own study of the Rosetta stone), Dr. Young was poring over a manuscript written hieroglyphics. Except for three names written in Greek character-Apollonius, Antigonus, and Antiochus (which he read as Antimachus)-he could make neither head nor tail of it. He put the papyrus away and in another shipment found another papyrus. This one proved to be written entirely in Greek. As Young scanned it quickly before putting it aside, his eye caught the same names that he had just read in the Egyptian manuscript, though in a slightly different form: Portis Apollonii and Antimachus Antigenis. With a shock, he realised that he had before him a translation of the hieroglyphs. Somehow, the document had survived for 2,000 years and, from and entirely different parts of the world, had come to him at the moment when it was most needed. Such a conspiracy of events, he wrote later, would have been quite sufficient , in an earlier age, to convince people that he had learned not only hieroglyphics but also the secrets of Egyptian sorcery.

98. Popal Coincidence

On 18th October, 1405, Pope Pius II was born; on the same day in 1417, Pope Gregory XII died, as did Pope Pius III in 1503.

99. Bald for 35 Years

In 1971, a long-distance truck driver, Edwin Robinson was left blind and almost deaf as a result of a bad road accident. Doctors gave him little hope of recovery and over the years, he learned to adapt to his afflictions. One day, with a storm brewing, he went into the backyard of his home in Maine to check on his pet chickens. As he passed a poplar tree, a bolt of lightning struck, knocking him unconscious.

Twenty minutes later, he returned to consciousness to discover he could see again — in fact, better than he had nine years earlier — and also his hearing was fully restored.

A month after the accident, there was an additional bonus. He told *The New York Times* how hair had begun to grow on his bald scalp. He had been bald for thirty-five years, believing it to be an hereditary condition, something he had to accept, like his blindness and deafness.

100. Common Lives

One of the most famous Time Twin case involved Samuel Hemming. He was born on the same day and at the same time as George III (4th June, 1738).

The commoner and the king were very much the same in appearance and their lives ran along similar lines – though, of course, at different levels. Hemming set up as an ironmonger on the day George succeeded to the throne.

Both were married on 8th September, 1761. They had the same number of children of the same sex, became ill and had accidents at the same time, and both died on 19th January, 1820 of similar causes.

George IV also had a mirror-image Time Twin, born within the same hour. The twin was only a lowly chimney sweep, but was equally renowned for gambling, philandering and spending, and both were addicted to racing. The prince raced thoroughbreds and the sweep donkeys. On the day the prince was kicked by a horse, his "twin" was kicked by a donkey. Both took the same amount of time to recover and when the prince went bankrupt, so did the sweep.

101. Two Births

On 7th November, 1984, Gail McClure and her sister, Carol Killian, gave birth to daughters within an hour of each other at Mesa's Lutheran Hospital in Arizona. Three years later, they did it again at the same hospital. On 11th February, 1987, Gail had a son, Benjamin. Forty-five minutes later, Carol had another girl, Christi, when the same doctor, who had delivered the first children, carried out a Caesarean section.

'After we did it the first time, we talked about doing it again,' said Gail. 'We tried to plan the due date in March but both got pregnant soon. Then we didn't talk about it, because we both thought we had ruined the plan.' It wasn't until they were both three months pregnant that they found out both were due at the same time again. Gail was due on the 1st of February and Carol, a week later. 'She waited for me,' said Carol. 'Is that amazing or what?'

102. Conceived at the Same Time

Three Kelley sisters of New York became pregnant at the same time in 1981 and, in February 1982, they gave birth within thirty-four hours of each other.

In 1982, Margaret Wright, twenty-seven, and her *older* sister, Dianne, twenty-nine, gave birth together. In October 1984, Margaret was back in hospital about to give birth again, as was her *younger* sister, Wendy, twenty-three. The two went into labour together but Margaret gave birth six hours earlier than Wendy — a boy, Samuel, weighing 4 kilos. Wendy had a girl, Heidi, weighing 3.35 kilos. The two sisters were put in a labour ward side by side, with the doctor running between the two. The women said the double births were entirely coincidental. 'It was a real surprise to me when I found out Wendy was pregnant,' said Margaret. 'We were actually due two weeks apart but we were both praying we'd have the babies together. When it came to the time, out prayers were answered — Wendy was a week later and I was a week early. We both went into labour together. It was a tremendous help to know Margaret was going through labour just as I was. I kept reassuring myself that I would get through it because Margaret was.'

103. Written on the Wind

Camille Flammarion, the celebrated 19th-century French astronomer, was also a student of the occult, in particular of how the appearance of ghosts might relate to the question of life after death. In his book, *The Unknown,* published in 1900, he records how, when he was writing the chapter on the wind

in his major work on the atmosphere (*L'Atmosphere*), a gale blew open his window, lifted the loose pages he had just written, and carried them off. A few days later, he was mystified to receive proof of the vanished chapter from his publisher. The wind had carried the papers into a street traversed by the publisher's porter, who often acted as a messenger of Flammarion. The porter had simply picked up the scattered pages of the chapter and taken them to the publisher in the usual way.

104. Crossword Puzzle

The Allied preparations for the invasion of Europe in 1944 were cloaked in unprecedented secrecy. Each phase of the operation, which was coded as 'Operation Overload', was

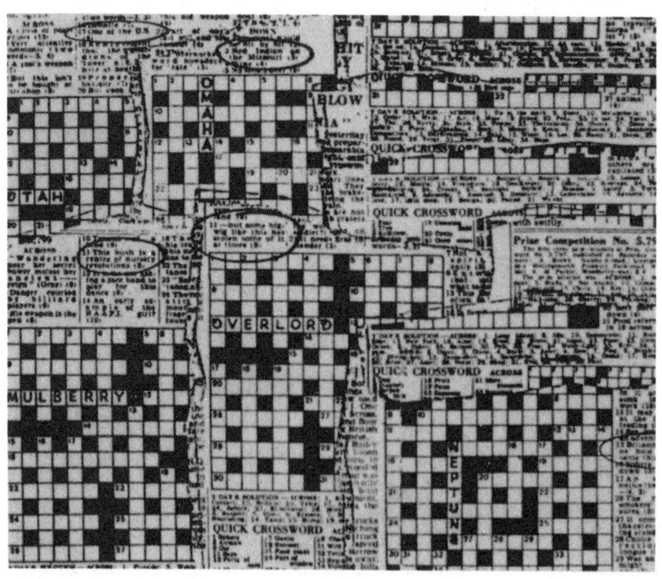

assigned its own code name. Among the most important of these were Neptune, code for the naval initiative, Omaha and Utah, the designations of two French beaches where landings were to take place, and Mulberry, the code name for the artificial harbours to be used for beachhead supply.

Thirty-three days before the scheduled date of the invasion, these code names began to crop up in the London *Daily Telegraph* crossword puzzle. On June 2, only four days before the invasion was launched, the code Overlord appeared, given as the solution for the clue reading "some big-wig like this has stolen some of it at times."

Security men descended on the *Telegraph's* Fleet Street offices, certain that a Nazi spy had given the game away. Instead, they found a bewildered schoolteacher named Leonard Dawe who had been compiling the paper's crossword puzzle for 20 years. He managed to convince the interrogators of his innocence: He had been guilty of nothing but an outrageous coincidence.

105. Canadian Mounted Police

As a young girl, Mrs C. L. Watt of Adelaide, South Australia, had always wanted to meet 'one of those glamorous Canadian Mounties.'

As an adult, she went to Canada, but after nearly three years there, she still had not fulfilled her wish. Then she had to travel from Vancouver to Toronto and took the Canadian Pacific Railway. One evening, in the crowded dining car, she was shown to the only vacant seat at a table for four. The other three were men, one in army uniform, the other a civilian and the third, a fair-haired young man looking resplendent in full Mountie uniform, scarlet jacket, etc.

The other two men struck up a conversation with her, but the tall, handsome Mountie, at first, just sat and listened then he spoke firmly, "You are an Australian?' Mrs Watt said she was. 'So am I!'

A royal Canadian Mounted Police officer who was an Australian! The coincidence grew when he asked, what part of Australia she had come from. He, too, came from Adelaide, and not only that but the same suburb, Semaphore.

'Of the many members of the Canadian Mounted Police the only one I had met in three years happened to be from my own home town,' she recalls. 'I am a very elderly citizen but I have often thought of that long-ago meeting with my Mountie.'

106. Greenberry Hill

The New York Herald reported on 26th November, 1911 that Sir Edmundbury Godfrey had been savagely done to death at a place called Greenberry Hill. The three men convicted of the crime and subsequently hanged were called Green, Berry and Hill.

107. Travelling Mates

Sara Roberts hitched a ride from the south coast of England back to London and was dropped off in an area she was not familiar with.

She was standing on the street trying to get her bearings when a door opened behind her and out came a good friend. The friend had moved flat a few weeks before and she had had no idea where he had gone.

Talking of friends . . . another friend of Sara booked into a hotel in Ireland and, as he was unpacking, found in one of the drawers a briefcase belonging to his brother (who had stayed in the room the previous night). The brothers lived more than 300 kilometres apart and rarely met.

108. Birthday Coincidences

As he bravely faced the fiery West Indian bowling attack, Australian cricketer Tim May had every reason to believe the coincidences surrounding him were a portent of victory.

It had been four years since May last played for Australia and his recall came for the Fourth Test of the 1992-93 series at the Adelaide Oval, his home ground.

On 25th January, May had taken an amazing five wickets for only nine runs - reason enough for him and his team mates to celebrate. With the West Indies all out for a lowly 185, victory looked certain.

May had another reason to celebrate: He had performed an amazing bowling feat on the eve of his thirty-first birthday. Now it was his birthday. By coincidence, it was also Australia's birthday, the 26th of January. However, fortune had taken a turn for the worst. The runs required to win were beginning to seem more and more elusive as Australian wickets fell cheaply.

In fact, the responsibility for winning the Test had fallen on Tim May, as on the previous day. Though other batsmen failed against the desperate West Indians (a defeat for them meant they would lose the series), May held out, his score gradually climbing.

Finally, with Craig McDermott joining May, Australia was down to its last wicket. Each ball bowled could see the end of the match.

May and McDermott stuck to their task of closing the gap. They were cool under fire, as an anxious nation watched.

Would the national day bring the appropriate victory? Could May celebrate his birthday as a national hero?

With tension almost unbearable, Australia reached 184, one run behind. The West Indians were rattled. Fortune had swung Australia's way.

However, a ball brushed past McDermott's gloves and the wicketkeeper caught it. The West Indies had won the narrowest victory in the long history of Test cricket.

Talking of Australia Day, a woman born on its fifteenth anniversary was named Leonore Australia Mullampy. In 1939 she married Lyndon Day. Since then she's been Mrs Australia day.

109. Valentine's Day

Judy Valentine gave birth to triplet sons, Rowan, Michael and Mark, on Valentine's Day, 1981. One hundred years to the day before this, the grandfather of the triplets, on the father, Steven's, side, was born. His name: Valentine Valentine.

The parents had not planned the triplets' birthday. In fact, the three were born by Caesarean section weeks before they were due.

110. Winning Numbers

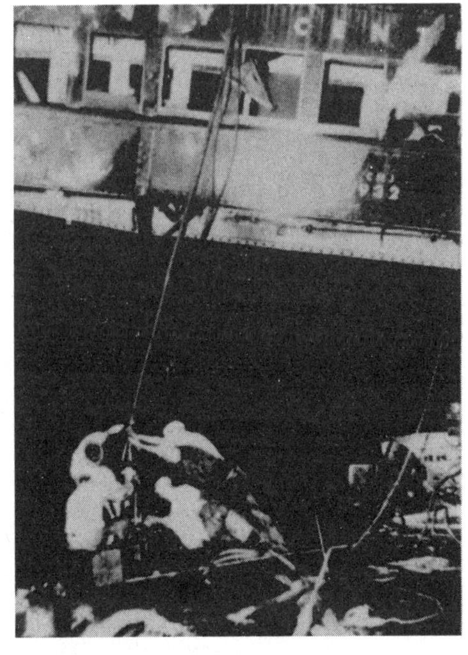

When the Jersey Central train plunged from a bridge into Newark Bay in 1958, cameramen rushed to the scene. One front-page newspaper photograph showed the rear coach being winched out of the water, with the number 932 clearly visible on its side. That day, 932 was the number chosen by thousands in the New York number game, and that day, 932 was the winning number.

111. Rare Parts

Best-selling author and pilot Richard Bach was barnstorming in the Midwest in 1966 with a rare biplane, a 1929 Detroit-Parks P-2a Speedster, only eight of which were ever built. In Palmyra, Wisconsin, Bach loaned the plane to a friend, who upended the craft as he came in for a landing. "They were able to fix everything except for one strut. That repair looked hopeless because of the rarity of the wanted part."

Just then the man, who owned the hangar near them, came up and asked if he might help, offering to let them have any of the bits and pieces stored in his three hangars. When Bach explained what rare parts he needed, the man walked over to a pile of junk and pointed to the parts. Bach concludes that

the odds against our breaking the biplane in a little town that happened to be home to a man with the forty-year-old part to repair it: the odds that he would be on the scene when the event happened; the odds that we'd push the plane right next to his hangar, within ten feet of the part we needed — the odds were so high that coincidence was a foolish answer.

112. The Toss of a Coin

Dr. Tom Leonard, a professor of statistics at the University of Warwick, England, provided the following observations and story to Arthur Koestler in 1974.

A particular coincidental event has, by definition, an infinitesimally small probability of occurring. However, there are infinitely many events which might possibly occur coincidentally to a particular person but, as it happens, do not occur. If we summed over all possible coincidental events, we would find the probability of at least one of them occurring during the person's lifetime to be quite sizable. I would, indeed, be surprised if many people could say that they had never experienced an extreme coincidence.

The best coincidence yarn I know runs as follows. In his first lecture at this university, a new professor of statistics was describing the laws of probability to his students. To illustrate them, he removed a coin from his pocket and tossed it in the air. It landed on a polished floor, spun around a few times, and to a thunderous applause came to rest — vertically on its edge! The point is that this was one of many coincidences that might have happened.

The chances of a (perfectly rounded) coin coming to rest on its edge after being tossed have been calculated by mathematician Warren Weaver at approximately one billion to one.

113. An Iceberg in the Sky

In July 1975, a large block of ice fell through the roof of the Melkis home in Dunstable, Bedford, England. At the time of the incident, the family was engrossed in a TV movie about the *Titanic.* As the ice crashed through their ceiling, they were tensely waiting for the ship to strike the fateful iceberg.

114. 7incoln 700

Significant '7' has long been attributed to Abraham Lincoln - the sixteenth (1 + 6 = 7) president of the US. Even if the following does stretch credulity, it shows one way of tracing a pattern of a personal number. Each of Lincoln's names contain seven letters. He lived seven years in Kentucky and seven years in Salem. In the army, he was a private (seven letters) and a captain (seven).

Lincoln was elected seven times, sworn into Congress on the 7th of December, 1847, held seven offices in succession. His ancestors came from Hingham (seven letters), in Norfolk (seven letters), England (seven letters). He served seven years in the state legislature. He appointed seven cabinet ministers, watched seven states secede and died a few minutes after seven on the seventh day.

115. The Third President

The third US president was dogged by the number, '3'. Thomas Jefferson was born on the 13th of April, 1743, the third child and the third Thomas in the family. He became the third president, but not before he largely wrote the *Declaration of Independence* at the age of thirty-three. And not before he lost the 1796 election by three votes.

Jefferson died at the age of eighty-three, on 4th July, 1826, the fiftieth anniversary of American Independence Day. The second American president, John Adams also died on that date. Incidentally, 4th July was significant for yet another president, Calvin Coolidge, the 30th president, who was born on 4th July, 1872.

116. The Lucky Survivors

In 1979, *Das Beste,* the German edition of *Reader's Digest,* ran a competition for the best story of a personal experience by one of its readers. The winner, chosen from 7,000 entries, was a pilot named Walter Kellner, of Munich. Kellner had described how his plane, a Cessna 421, had crashed into the Tyrrhenian Sea between Sardinia and Sicily and how he had survived the ordeal in a rubber dinghy. *Digest* researchers checked the story carefully against the German and Italian reports of the accident and satisfied themselves that Kellner's account was true. His Cessna, registration number D-INUR, had indeed plunged 10,000 feet to the bottom of the Tyrrhenian Sea as he described.

The date of the prize giving was set for December 6, and Kellner was to bring the rubber dinghy to the *Das Beste* offices.

On the morning of the presentation, a letter arrived at *Das Beste* for Editor-in-Chief Wulf Schwarzwaller, who was to hand Kellner his prize. The letter was from Walter Kellner-another Walter Kellner, who lived in Kritzendorg, Austria. This Kellner was also a pilot. The story was fake, he said. He had flown that same Cessna for four years over Europe and the Mediterranean, and though he had once had to make a forced landing with engine trouble at the Cagliari airstrip in Sardinia, he had never once gone down at sea. Some impostor had taken his story, invented a new ending, and was about to make off with the prize money.

Schwarzwaller was dumbfounded. How could this be when the story had been so carefully checked? And what to do now? The author of the story was due to arrive for lunch soon. . .

Just as scheduled, a smiling Walter Kellner arrived at the *Das Beste* office, was welcomed, and then promptly shown the letter from his namesake.

At first, he laughed. Yes, he knew from the plane's records that another Kellner had flown it, but he had had no idea that they shared same first name. Then he came to the part of the letter describing the other Kellner's forced landing in Sardinia-and turned pale. The same plane, the same area, the same engine problem, and a pilot with the same name. What jinx had been at work? Why should the Cessna seem to have a grudge against Walter Kellners, and why should it apparently - have been determined to destroy itself and its pilot, in the vicinity of the Tyrrhenian Sea?

The questions were unanswerable. The two Walter Kellners had been touched by a mystery that they were lucky to survive. The *Das Beste* editors had unwittingly nudged open a door onto the unknown, and through it, they could feel blowing, throughout the presentation, a chill and eerie wind.

117. The 13th Day of a Month

An artist, who believed his death was predetermined by his birth date, was the Austrian composer, Arnold Schoenberg.

Born on 13th September, 1874, he believed he would die on the thirteenth day of a month. Schoenberg, noted for his origination of the twelve-note technique, further believed that as the number 7 and 6 make 13, he would die at the age of seventy-six. He died thirteen minutes before midnight on Friday, the 13th of July, 1951. His age was seventy-six.

118. Number 17

King John III of Poland was born on the 17th of June. It was also the date on which he ascended the throne, the date on which he married and the date on which he died.

119. The Fishy Stench

On Midsummer Eve, 1626, a Mr. Mead of Christ's College, Cambridge, England, was walking through the city marketplace when he heard a commotion coming from a fishmonger's stall. A small crowd had gathered and was examining a book that the fisherwoman had just discovered inside a large codfish:

I saw all with my own eyes [Mr. Mead wrote]-the fish, the maw [stomach], the piece of sailcloth, the book-and observed all I have written. What I did not see was the opening of the fish, which not many did, being on the fisherwoman's stall in the market, who first cut off its head, to which the maw was hanging, and seeming much stuffed with somewhat, it was searched, and all found as aforesaid. He that had had his nose as near as I yester morning would have been persuaded there was no imposture here without witness. The fish came from Lynn [King's Lynn, in Norfolk]

The book which Mr. Mead took charge of, had been bound in sailcloth and, though slimy and dog-eared, was perfectly legible. It proved to be a theological treatise written by John Frith during his imprisonment at Oxford, a hundred years before. So highly did the Cambridge authorities think of this remarkable mode of book distribution that they had the volume reprinted under the title, *Vox Piscis* ('the voice of the fish') *or*, the *Bookfish*, and embellished it with an engraving of the fish, the book, and the fishmonger's knife.

Young Frith had been imprisoned in a cellar where fish were stored and where the stench was so great that several of his fellow prisoners had actually died of it. Frith himself was burned at the stake as a heretic in 1533.

120. Four Principles

Angie Hartnell and Ricky Todd, who had lived four miles apart for years, were both born on 4th October, 1954. They met on 4th October, 1979, were engaged on 4th October, 1980 and married on 4th October, 1982. They had four bridesmaids and four ushers at the church in Silverton, Devon. They said that the October 4 events in their lives were coincidences. They hoped to have four children.

121. Twin Lives

Twins, of course, have most chance of being involved in coincidences between themselves. But Chris and Christine Mikhael and their family have been more than surprised at the coincidences that have occurred so far in their young lives, especially by the sudden prediction made by their mother when their all-important Higher School Certificate examination reports arrived at their home on 11th January, 1989. Before they had had a chance to open the envelopes, their mother said: "I bet you'll score the same." Moments later, her prediction was proved correct.

Given the broad range of marks and the numbers of people involved in crediting them, the result can only be considered highly coincidental. Had they come within a few points of one another, it would have been remarkable.

Chris and Christine were born within half and hour of one another in 1970. Both attended the same school; Chris was captain and Christine, the vice-captain. In 1986, the two had been scalded by oil, in different locations but at the same time of the day, Chris while on a camping holiday and Christine while filling in for Chris at his part-time job at a takeaway food bar. Chris says he and his sister often have the same thoughts: "I'll say something" and Christine will say, "I was just thinking of that."

122. Breath Test Machine

In 1984, the police booked Julia McArdie for failing a breath test — the machine had been invented by her father.

123. Nine Lives

Jessica Lee Bromwell was born at nine minutes past nine on the ninth day of the ninth month in 1990, which means she turns nine on the ninth day of the ninth month in 1999.

124. A Rebirth Symbol

Carl Gustave Jung, one of the founding fathers of the 20th century psychology, told the following story in his treatise "Synchronicity: An Acausal Connecting Principle," written in 1960:

A young woman, I was treating, had dream in which she was given a golden scarab.

While she was telling me this dream, I sat with my back to the closed window. Suddenly, I heard a noise behind me, like a gentle tapping. I turned around and saw a flying insect knocking against the windowpane from the outside. I opened the window and caught the creature in the air as it flew in. It was the nearest analogy to a golden scarab that one finds in out latitudes, a scarabaeid beetle, the common rose-chafer (*Cetonia aurata),* which contrary to its usual habits had evidently felt an urge to get into a dark room at this particular moment. . . .

There ... seems to be an archetypal foundation to the ...case. It was an extraordinarily difficult case to treat, and up to the time of the dream little or no progress had be made. I should explain that the main reason for this was my patient's animus, which.... clung so rigidly to its own idea of reality that three doctors — I was the third-had not been able to weaken it. Evidently, something quite irrational was needed which was beyond my powers to produce. The dream alone was enough to disturb the rationalistic attitude of my patient. But when the "scarab" came flying in through the window in actual fact, her natural being could burst through the armour of her animus possession and the process of transformation could at last begin to move. Any essential change of attitude signifies a psychic renewal which is usually accompanied by symbols of rebirth in the patient's dreams and fantasies. The scarab is a classic example of a rebirth symbol.

125. Twittering Movements

The English novelist, J.B. Priestley, who is married to the well-known archaeologist, Jacquetta Hawks, related this experience to Arthur Koestler in a letter dated February 7, 1972:

My wife bought three large lithographs by Graham Sutherland. When they arrived here from London, she took them up to her bedroom, to hang them up in the morning. They were leaning against a chair and the one on the outside, facing the room was a lithograph of a grasshopper. When Jacquetta got into bed that night, she felt some sort of twittering movement going on, so she got out and pulled back the clothes. There was a grasshopper in the bed. No grasshopper had been seen in that room before, nor has been seen since. No grasshopper has been seen at any other time in this house.

126. Cry of Wild Goose

As Noel McCabe, of Derby, England, was listening to a record of Frankie Laine singing, "Cry of the Wild Goose," in 1974, a Canada goose crashed through his bedroom window and two more fell to the ground outside.

127. Time of Death

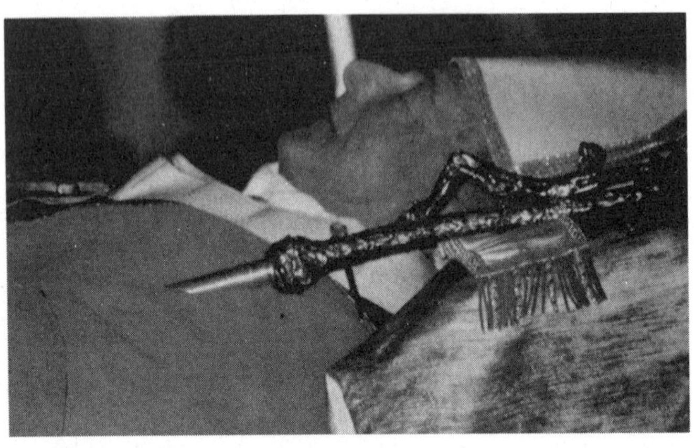

Pope Paul VI was presented with an alarm clock in 1923. It served him faithfully for 55 years, waking him promptly at 6 o'clock every morning. On Sunday, 6th August, 1978, the alarm clock rang, apparently of its own accord, at 9.40 p.m. — it was the very moment that the Pope died.

128. It Ceased Raining

San Francisco judge Samuel King, annoyed that jurors were unable to make it to court because of continual heavy rain, issued a decree: 'I hereby order that it cease raining by Tuesday.'

That was in 1986 and drought hit California for the next five years. In 1991, he was reminded of his decree by colleagues and proclaimed: "I hereby rescind my order of 18th February, 1986 and order that rain shall fall in California beginning from 27th February."

On that day, a fierce storm swept over the Pacific, drenching the state with more than 100 millimetres of rain. In the next few days, two smaller storms added more rain. Squalls continued for the next fortnight.

129. Book of Chance

Dame Rebecca West, the novelist and historian, was in the library of the Royal institute of International Affairs in London, looking for a particular piece of information.

After a long and fruitless search, she finally gave up. 'It's pointless searching!' she said to the librarian, pointing to the hundreds of volumes of the court proceedings. The information I want could be in any of these books!' To emphasise her point, she picked one of the books from the shelf and opened it. There, in front of her, was the information she had been looking for!

130. Identical Tattoos

In the early hours of 20th May 1988, a train hit a nineteen-year-old youth, while he was walking on the tracks. The police searched the man's shredded clothing for some identity and found the address of a young woman. Assuming it to be that of the man's girlfriend, they went to the address, which was near the scene of the accident, and asked her to describe her boyfriend. She did so, including details of his height, colour of hair and tattoos and other body markings. 'She described him to a T,' said an officer. She also gave them the address of the boy. When the police went there, the boyfriend's parents said their son was asleep in his bed. Through an amazing coincidence, the son had identical tattoos and body-markings to the train victim, a case of the wind of coincidence blowing both good and ill omens.

131. The Bizarre Story

The circumstances of the above incident only add to the bizarre nature of a similar story which began with Arthur Keostler when he wrote an article on coincidences for the *Sunday Times.* As a follow-up, the newspaper offered a £100 prize for the reader who submitted the best coincidence.

The winner was Nigel Parker, aged twelve, who told a story that demands comparison with the story told by Law, all those years before. Parker's story was of his great-grandfather's cousin, a cabin boy on a yawl, the *Mignonette,* which foundered in 1884. The boy and three senior crew members managed to launch an open boat. They were the only survivors. The three men eventually ate the boy, whose name was Richard Parker.

The case was reported in *The Times* of 28th October, 1884. In 1838, Edgar Allan Poe had written a story called 'The Narrative of Arthur Gordon Pym of Nantucket'. Poe tells a similar story of shipwreck and a cabin boy survivor who is also eaten by the other survivors. His name was Richard Parker!

132. Important

Number 7 has played an important part in the life of Dianne Randall's family. They lived in a house with a street number, 7. The family — five children, two parents — totalled seven. Her eldest brother was born on 7th July, 1943, her second brother on 7th May, 1945, the third brother on 7th August, 1948, and she herself was born on 7th March, 1950. Her youngest brother was born on her third eldest brother's birthday, the 7th of August, 1952.

133. Highway 94

In 1987, Mexican-American Francisco Sandoval, forty-six, was killed when his car overturned on a bend on Highway 94, between San Diego, California, and the Mexican border.

Thirty-six hours later, a hearse carrying his body was involved in an accident on the same bend.

134. Fateful Reunion

Pratt Whitfield, a fifty-five-year-old disabled merchant seaman, was sitting on a park bench in the tough Bronx district, minding his own business, when he heard a fellow bench-sitter talking to a friend about a robbery they were planning for that night. When they mentioned that they planned to use a shotgun that one of them was carrying, Whitfield pricked up his ears. He rose from the bench as casually as possible and walked to a nearby police station.

Whitfield did more than report a planned robbery. Five years previously, two men had broken into his home. One had held a knife to his throat, the other aimed a shotgun at his wife. They had robbed the couple and had never been caught. But Whitfield had never forgotten the menacing voice of the robber. As he returned to the scene with two cops in tow, he confronted them.

'Do you remember me?' Whitfield asked thirty-three-year-old James King. 'You robbed me and my wife five years ago with that gun!'

There was no menace in King's voice as he faced Whitfield this time. In fact, King was speechless. He gave up without a struggle and was sent to stand trial for a number of robberies, including the Whitfield job. King had a long list of convictions.

The story does not end there. The stature of limitations for robbery runs for five years and this fateful reunion at the park bench happened *the day before* the five-year limitation on the Whitfield robbery was up.

135. Hitler and Chaplin's Mo

An observer has traced significant coincidences between Hitler and Charlie Chaplin! Professor Hary Geduld of Indiana University points out the coincidences between the dictator and the comic began with the proximity of their births. Chaplin was born on 16th April, 1889, in London and Hitler, four days later, in Braunau-am-Inn, Austria.

Geduld, a prolific author and professor of comparative literature, notes that both were born into working-class families and both had bullying fathers whom they detested, and sickly, indulgent mothers whom they adored.

As young men, they had artistic aspirations. Chaplin wanted to be England's greatest dramatic actor, Hitler a great painter. Each grew into temperamental adults given to unpredictable, sometimes, terrifying tantrums.

But, says Geduld, the most striking coincidence was their celebrated moustaches. Hitler imitated Chaplin in this, whether he was aware of it or not. Chaplin adopted the moustache in his second film, *Kid's Auto Race* (1914), while Hitler did not trim his moustache into its famous shape until after the First World War, by which time Chaplin had appeared in dozens of movies with his distinctive tache. Geduld says Hitler's motivation for adopting the most famous 'trademark' of a man who exemplified all that he most abhorred is a mystery.

136. Fellow of King's College

In the August 1991 edition of *Locus* magazine, Arthur C. Clarke wrote of a coincidence that must have helped cheer him up during his recovery from an operation he underwent at the University College Hospital, London, for the removal of a massive diverticulum (bladder extension) and prostate. The operation lasted two-and-a-half hours, was difficult and he lost five pints of blood. When he woke up, he found himself with three tubes inserted at strategic spots.

A few weeks after returning home to Colombo, Sri Lanka, he came across a passage in Ronald Clark's *JBS: The Life of J.B.S. Haldane* (1968).

Haldane returned to London during the early part of November [1963]. Rather reluctantly, he entered the University College Hospital ... an operation was necessary ... when he recovered consciousness from the anaesthetic, Haldane wrote to Arthur Clarke, the noted writer of science fiction, he became aware of three tubes which had been inserted into him.

'I was fed through one into a vein, another went via my nose to my stomach ... the third was a urethral catheter, which I considered a great luxury. To judge from some S.F. [science

fiction] this is a foretaste of the future. What little is left of our natural bodies is to be attached to a variety of gadgets.

Clarke says he had completely forgotten this letter. Reading the passage twenty-seven years later gave him 'a most peculiar feeling'. As he said: 'To have woken up in the same place, with the same number of tubes in me as JBS, certainly does seem to strain the bounds of probability. And there was no way the choice of location could have been an unconscious self-fulfilling prophecy. UCH was chosen by my surgeon … and, in fact, as a Fellow of King's College, I feel guilty of defecting to a rival establishment.

■■■

References

1. Dumas Malone, The Sage of Monticello, Vol. 6, pp. 497-98.
2. Augustus J.C. Hare, The Story of My Life, Vol. 1, pp. 383-84.
3. Ken Anderson, Coincidences – Chance or Fate ?, 1995.
4. Sue Balckhall, The World's Greatest Blunders, 1987.
5. Corrine Kenner et al, Strange but True, 1997.
6. Peter Eldin, Amazing Mysteries of the Unexplained, 1987.
7. Richard Marshall, Mysteries of the Unexplained, 1987.
8. Repleys, Giant Book of Believe it or Not.
9. Joseph Bryan III, The Sword Over the Mantel, quoted in Holiday, Nov. 1962, p.50.
10. Alan Vaugham, Incredible Coincidences, 1981.
11. Ken Anderson, Coincidences : Accidents or Design, 1991.
12. Emile Borel, Probability and life, 1961.
13. John Fairley, Arthur C. Clarke's World of Strange Powers, 1984.
14. Camille Flammarion, The Unknown, 1990, p.194.
15. Arthur Koestler, The Challenge of Chance, 1973.
16. John May, Curious Facts, 1984.

17. Robert L. Ripley, Believe it or Not, Pocket series, 1964.
18. Danah Zohar, Through the Time Barrier, 1983.
19. Colin Wilson, The Psychic Detectives, 1984.
20. Colin Wilson, Strange Powers, 1973.
21. Lyall Watson, The Gift of Unknown Things, 1976.
22. Holiday, November 1962, p.52.
23. The Unexplained : Mysteries of Mind, Space and Time, Series.
24. Ripley's Ghost Stories and Plays, pp. 30-33.
25. Scientific American, October 19, 1972, p.110.
26. Martin Gardner, The Incredible Dr. Matrix, pp. 42-45.
27. The Sunday Times (London), May 5, 1974.
28. Luiggi Gedda and Gianni Brianni, Chronogenetic : The Inheritance of Biological Time.
29. Rickard M., Phenomena : A Book of Wonders, p. 90
30. Readers Digest, January 1980, p.78.
31. Official History of Guilford Vermont, 1678-1961, p.94.
32. Thomas Young, An Account of some Research Discoveries in Hieroglyphical Literature and Egyptian Antiquities, pp. 55-58.
33. International Journal of Parapsychology, 10:223-224, 1968.
34. Courier, April 1980, pp. 12-13.
35. Roll W.6, Morris R.S, Morris J.D., Eds. Research in Parapsychology p. 209.
36. Readers Digest, Mysteries of the Unexplained.
37. Roger L. Williams, Gaslight and Shadows, pp. 156-57.

38. Readers Digest, August 1979, p.120.
39. Nature, 258:466-468, December 11, 1975.
40. Noel Nouet, Histoire de Tokyo, p.98.
41. Edward H. Sothern, My Remembrances "The Melancholy Tale of "Me", p.341.
42. Horald Nicolson, Small Talk, pp.99-101.
43. Alexander Woollcott, While Rome Burns, pp.20-23.
44. Goodman Linda, Star Signs, 1987.
45. Readers Digest, Into the Unknown, 1982.
46. Ripley, Robert L., The Book of Chances, 1989.
47. Colin Wilson, The Occult, 1971.
48. Jung, Karl, Synchronicity, 1960.
49. Koestler, Arthur, The Roots of Coincidence, 1972.
50. Huff, Darrell, How to take a chance, 1959.
51. Inglis, Brain, Coincidences: A Matter of Chance or Synchronicity?, 1990.

■■■

Unexplained Mysteries